THE ONLINE CATALOG:

IMPROVING PUBLIC
ACCESS TO
LIBRARY MATERIALS

by Emily Gallup Fayen

Knowledge Industry Publications, Inc.
White Plains, NY and London

Professional Librarian Series

The Online Catalog: Improving Public Access to Library Materials

Library of Congress Cataloging in Publication Data

Fayen, Emily Gallup.
    The online catalog.

    (Professional librarian series)
    Bibliography: p.
    Includes index.
    1. Catalogs, On-line   2. On-line bibliographic searching.   3. Library catalogs and readers.   4. Libraries—Automation.   I. Title.   II. Series.
    Z699.F34   1983   025.3'028'54   83-12009
    ISBN 0-86729-054-4
    ISBN 0-86729-053-6 (soft)

Printed in the United States of America

10   9   8   7   6   5   4   3   2   1

Table of Contents

List of Tables and Figures

1

What Is an Online Catalog?

The online catalog is changing forever the way people use their libraries. No longer is it necessary to sort laboriously through endless indexes, card files, listings and bibliographies to locate information. Instead, people can use the computer to sort quickly through mountains of raw data to get at facts and figures. For over two decades, people working in specific disciplines such as medicine, chemistry, the social sciences and law have been able to take advantage of computer-based information retrieval. As computers become increasingly affordable, and as library automation becomes commonplace, most libraries will be able to offer online catalogs to their patrons. However, the transition may not be an easy one. Although the trend is clear, libraries face difficult decisions and radical change if they are to bring this about.

LIBRARIES IN THE AGE OF INFORMATION

Libraries are at a critical point in their history. They have tremendous investments in their existing collections, catalog card files and manual procedures. But society will not wait for libraries to accommodate themselves gradually to the changing world of computer technology. The "Information Age" is here to stay, and libraries must join the mainstream of progress or find themselves slowly eddying around in a backwash of antiquated products and services.

Early warnings of the impending crisis have been with us for some time. In a 1961 address entitled "A Library for 2000 A.D.," John Kemeny noted:

> ...it is clear that the library of the future will have to make heavy use of automation. There is no conceivable way in a library of several tens of millions of volumes that human effort could locate an item in a matter of minutes.[1]

---

1. John G. Kemeny, "A Library for 2000 A.D.," *M.I.T. Centennial Lecture Series* (Cambridge, MA: March 27, 1961).

Here lies the crux of the problem: it is simply too costly and too time-consuming for libraries and their patrons to continue to provide (and to use) traditional library services in the traditional way. Thus, both users and providers of information have turned to computer technology for assistance in overcoming this problem. In fact, computer scientists envisioned this use of computers long before the technology existed to make automated library systems truly feasible or cost-effective. The history of the development of computer systems is dotted with attempts to solve library problems of one sort or another. There have been some remarkable successes—the Online Computer Library Center (OCLC), the Medical Literature and Retrieval System (MEDLARS)—and some notable failures. Both have served to demonstrate to users and providers of library services alike that the task is not a simple one.

EVOLUTION OF LIBRARY AUTOMATION

The move toward library automation occurred in three major phases. In the first phase, which began in the mid-1960s, computers were used as high-speed typewriters in the processing of library materials. The earliest efforts were in catalog card production and the preparation of book catalogs and microform catalogs. This use of computers in libraries permitted extraordinarily labor-intensive tasks to be performed more rapidly and cheaply, and with a much lower error rate. Further, by producing book and microform catalogs the library could make its catalog available in more than just the one card catalog location.

Rise of Bibliographic Utilities

The next step came when libraries realized that they could save even more if they shared the cost of cataloging their materials. Thus, in the early 1970s, OCLC and a few other vendors began to offer shared cataloging services via online linkup to a central data base. These service bureaus—not to be confused with the earlier abstracting and indexing services that emerged during the 1960s—became known as *bibliographic utilities*. They have formed the foundation of all subsequent library automation projects.

The shared cataloging services allowed libraries to convert their card catalogs to machine-readable form. Once machine-readable, the data could then be used as the basic data file for a large number of library operations, including the online catalog.

Automated Library Systems

The third major phase in library automation occurred when library administrators began to realize that the computer could also be used to automate many of the tedious, expensive record-keeping functions involved in the daily operation of a library: namely circulation, acquisitions and serials receipt control. This phase of library automation has been of tremendous benefit to the libraries that have participated in it because, for the most part, the systems that have been installed have contributed to cost containment and have made valuable management information available to library decision makers.

But this phase of library automation, beneficial as it is, has been aimed mainly at the library staff. Although users have received better service because of online circulation systems, none of the automated library functions comprising this phase has given the user much assistance in locating information.

THE CONCEPT OF ONLINE ACCESS

The term most often used to describe the type of user assistance needed is *online access*. This is a term that has been used (and misused) by numerous writers in the field, including myself, without being defined very well. Online access represents an entirely different method of getting information. It does *not* mean taking the conventional library card catalog and putting it, as it stands, on the computer. To quote from one of the early definitions of an online catalog, "...it is not just an outboard motor on a covered wagon."[2]

The distinction between online access and the conventional card catalog cannot be overstated. The most noticeable difference between the two is the speed of online information retrieval. However, more crucial are the underlying differences in the operation of the conventional and the online catalog. While the two may appear nearly identical—for example, the record displayed can look the same—user access to data is entirely different with the online catalog.

Rapid Retrieval of Information

Because it is the simplest, let us address the question of speed first. The interpretation of online information retrieval as a while-you-wait operation is the classic distinction between manual and automated retrieval systems. As applied to information retrieval systems, the term online means that the user can interact with the system directly and in *real time*.

The term "real time" comes from the earliest days of computer technology. The first computers were used to perform the long series of calculations needed to guide missiles and rockets. As missile technology improved and computers became more sophisticated, it became possible to guide such devices in flight; that is, a computer could be used to make real-time course corrections that would enable the missile to change course rapidly enough to match the changing course of its target. This led to the development of the first real-time computers.

The term real time means performing an operation so quickly that the results are available in time to be used to control some other process. Other examples of real-time processes are landing an airplane by remote control, flow process controls in oil refineries and chemical plants, and airplane reservations systems.

Interactive Retrieval

Online catalogs, then, are actually *real-time interactive retrieval systems for libraries*; that is, they are systems in which the user is connected directly to the information source (the catalog) and in which system responses occur quickly enough to enable the search request to be modified dynamically as the session progresses.

---

2. Ibid.

DEFINING THE ONLINE CATALOG

Although online access can be defined rather precisely, exactly what constitutes an online catalog is not yet clear. At the Dartmouth conference, sponsored by the Council on Library Resources in the summer of 1980,[3] the participants were asked to contribute a definition of an online catalog. The following samples show the wide variations among the definitions submitted:

[An online catalog provides] online access to the complete bibliographic record of all of the Library's holdings with minimal access points being the same as those available in a card catalog.
(National Library of Medicine)

———————————————

An online catalog:

• Provides the public with direct access to a library's bibliographic data base through the use of a terminal.

• Is searchable through a variety of access points greater than those available through card form catalogs.

• Is searchable with a common command language which may be transferred when the public moves from one library to another.

• Retrieves information from a local library file, and if not successful locally, retrieves information from other libraries' files.

• Provides instructional help.

• Displays search results in readily understandable form.

• Provides links to card form catalogs, reference help, circulation files, etc.

• May be accessed remote from the library's location.
(Research Libraries Group)

———————————————

An online catalog is an access tool and resource guide to the collections of a library or libraries, which contains interrelated sets of bibliographic data in machine-readable form and which can be searched interactively on a terminal by users.
(Library of Congress)

———————————

3. Council on Library Resources, Inc., "On-line Public Access to Library Bibliographic Data Bases: Developments, Issues, and Priorities," OCLC, Inc. and The Research Libraries Group, Inc. (September 1980).

A true "On-line Public Catalog" should provide sophisticated access for unsophisticated patrons. It should remove from the patron the burden of any interpretation of library procedures and practices.
(Pennsylvania State University)

An on-line catalogue implies access to the bibliographic description of the resources held by the Library. Such access should be via terminals fully available at all times, in several locations throughout the Library and throughout the university community.

In addition to the access provided for material currently held, the on-line catalogue should also reflect material both on order and in process.
(University of Guelph)

An online catalog is a system that provides online access to an organized body of information. Assuming that a library catalog has certain characteristics, an online replacement of that catalog must at least replicate the positive characteristics by providing the same types of access points and by serving the same volume of catalog users without requiring a greater investment of time or energy by those users. These minimum requirements are sufficient to provide a definition but the goal of an online catalog design should be to allow continual enhancement to the above characteristics to provide easier, more comprehensive access to information.
(University of Texas)

The essential elements of an online catalog, then, are:

• A full bibliographic record following MARC and other relevant standards, including acceptable subject headings;

• Access to the full record by at least the conventional access points used in the card catalog;

• A cross-reference structure, based upon an authority control structure;

• A patron interface that is at least as cordial as the card catalog;

• A detailed holdings and circulation record linked to the full bibliographic record;

• As many terminals as we can afford.
(University of Illinois)

An online catalog is a configuration of computer hardware and software that permits a library's users to interact quickly and efficiently with a file of machine-readable descriptions of library materials. The system is designed in such a way that patrons with no data processing knowledge can search both for items they are very familiar with and items they know very little about. Access to these items is offered in a variety of ways, including as an absolute minimum main entry, title, added entries and subject approaches.
(New York University)

While perhaps no one definition by itself provides an adequate description of an online catalog, collectively they do represent the thoughts of a great number of concerned librarians and online catalog systems designers regarding the nature of an online catalog.

Many of these definitions are couched in terms of the card catalogs with which we are all familiar. Many of them attempt to define an online catalog as at least providing the capabilities of the card catalog but having additional features. The drawback to this approach to defining any new system is that the new system may inadvertently incorporate features of the old that are not only unnecessary, but in fact, undesirable. As Douglas Ferguson of the Stanford University Library has pointed out, "We must be on the lookout for the buggy-whip holder!"

The definitions presented here were written in 1980, but as of 1983 there is still little consensus as to what an online catalog really is. In fact, how an online catalog is defined and what features it must (or should) have vary widely depending on who is writting the definition. Public services librarians and those who are involved in technical processing will often have quite different ideas as to what an online catalog is while systems designers may have still other notions.

FEATURES OF THE ONLINE CATALOG

What features should an online catalog have? As we shall see, the simplest, shortest definitions are probably the best, for they stipulate what the online catalog is to do and how the user will interact with it rather than attempting to specify how the system will accomplish these objectives.

Early in 1980, a group of librarians and systems designers who were interested in online catalogs met in Chicago to discuss a cooperative effort to develop an online catalog. This Consortium to Develop an Online Catalog, or CONDOC as it came to be called, represented about 125 medium-sized university and small college libraries who wanted to work together to develop a product to meet their needs. The CONDOC libraries require a reliable, flexible, computer-based integrated library system. The objective of the CONDOC online catalog is "to improve patron access to the library's collection and in turn make the resources of the library as widely accessible as possible.[4]

CONDOC (with the assistance of Joseph R. Matthews) developed a list of "Features of an Online Catalog" which they could use to specify the desired system. Each CONDOC member was asked to rank the features in order of importance. A list of 40 features was developed. They are listed below as ranked by the CONDOC group:

1. The system must be reliable with less than 2% unscheduled downtime.

2. The data base shall contain MARC format records for monographs, serials and other classes of materials.

---

4. Consortium to Develop an Online Catalog (CONDOC), "Specifications for an Online Catalog" (Chicago: November 2, 1981).

3. The data base must be searchable by author, title, subject and call number as a minimum.

4. Authority file cross-references must be provided as well as the ability to maintain the authority file information.

5. The system must provide keyword access to subject headings and titles.

6. The system must support an authority file for names and subject headings with appropriate cross-references.

7. The bibliographic citation must contain copy location information.

8. The system must use a standard CRT terminal with a user-friendly interface incorporating a menu display and/or a command language.

9. The response time must average less than five seconds with a maximum of 10 seconds.

10. The data base must contain citations for monographs and serials at a minimum.

11. The data base must be searchable by series entry.

12. The system must provide keyword searching for the title field.

13. The system must be expandable; that is, it must be able to accommodate more citations and more users.

14. The system should be capable of providing several different types of citation displays (e.g., brief record, full record and various indexes).

15. The system must provide Boolean operators for search refinement.

16. The data base must be searchable by author and title added entries.

17. The online catalog must have a system interface with other components of an integrated library system to provide on-order information.

18. The online catalog must have a system interface with the circulation system so that patrons can get location and status information.

19. The system should provide browsing capabilities over any file.

20. Numbers such as ISBN, ISSN, LC card number and so forth should be searchable.

21. The system must provide an Authority Control File for names and subject headings with no cross-references.

22. The system should be able to consist of the online catalog portion alone.

23. The system must provide some flexibility with respect to which portions of the MARC record are included and which fields are searchable.

24. The online catalog must have a system interface with other portions of the integrated library system and other external systems.

25. The cost must be reasonable.

26. The online catalog must provide a user interface with a command language only.

27. The authority file system will eliminate blind cross-references.

28. The system must be able to display the full MARC character set.

29. The system should allow some flexibility in displaying information on the CRT with respect to format.

30. The system should be able to display the full MARC record with tags and subfield indicators.

31. The user must be able to get a printout of the information displayed on the CRT.

32. The system must have an online link to a bibliographic utility for searching and displaying records.

33. The user interface must have a menu display only.

34. The publication date must be searchable.

35. The system must support some type of "fuzzy matching" to avoid problems caused by misspellings and differences in transliteration.

36. The system must provide some flexibility in the arrangement of citation information; i.e., retrieved citations should be sortable in a variety of ways.

37. The edition statement must be searchable.

38. The publisher information must be searchable.

39. The user interface need have a touch screen only.

40. The language of the item must be searchable.

Although this ranking is helpful in understanding the perceived needs of librarians and systems designers in developing online catalogs, it is far from being a specification of just what an online catalog is or should be. Rather, this list gives an idea of the importance that librarians attach to many of the factors involved in implementing an online catalog. What is needed now, however, is a definition of an online catalog that can be used as the basis for developing the much-needed list of desired specifications. I like best the definition proposed by the National Library of Medicine (NLM):

> [An online catalog provides] online access to the complete bibliographic record of all of the Library's holdings with minimal access points being the same as those available in a card catalog.

This definition has the advantage of brevity. It tells (in functional terms) what the online catalog is supposed to do, without getting bogged down in the details of implementation. Furthermore, it clearly indicates that the online catalog is an access tool rather than something else. That is, the online catalog is not an online cataloging system nor is it necessarily a mechanism for authority control. In the simplest possible terms, *the online catalog is a mechanism for providing real-time interactive access to the bibliographic records for a library's holdings. The online catalog provides for searching the bibliographic records in a variety of ways which need not be stipulated during data base creation, and which may be constructed by the user to meet a particular information need at the time the search is conducted.*

The remainder of this chapter will examine this definition in more detail and show why it makes the online catalog so vastly different from its predecessor.

DIFFERENCES BETWEEN ONLINE AND CONVENTIONAL CATALOGS

As noted, the most obvious difference between the online catalog and the conventional catalog is speed. However, there are other subtle but substantive differences between them.

Precoordinated Retrieval in the Conventional Catalog

Conventional library catalogs are *alphabetic* or *alphabetic-classed*. This means that the entries in the catalog are arranged in a predetermined order specified by the alphabet and the library's filing rules. A library catalog may interfile all entries so that personal names, corporate names, titles, series entries and subject headings are all arranged in one continuous alphabetic file. The advantage of this approach is that, leaving aside the vagaries introduced by filing rules, there is one order throughout the entire catalog and hence, one place to look for any single entry.

The subject portion of the library catalog is often also alphabetic-classed. This means that in addition to the main subject heading, subdivisions or subclasses have been established. For example,

UNITED STATES—FOREIGN RELATIONS—CHINA
VERMONT—DESCRIPTION AND TRAVEL

Within each of these subject classifications, the catalog cards are arranged by main entry. The subject headings (and subclassifications) are assigned at the time the item is being cataloged, and the library user is expected to locate desired materials by using the same guidelines and thought processes that governed the choice of heading during the cataloging process. This is called *precoordinated retrieval*. It means that the most desirable retrieval points for the item are selected at the time the bibliographic citation is being prepared. An attempt is made to predict how library users will want to locate a particular item in the future and the necessary access points are assigned at the outset.

There are two major difficulties with this approach. According to Sharp, "The failure of conventional systems is due virtually entirely to the impossibility of providing the necessary number of entries to facilitate retrieval in all cases by one-place reference to a file in known order."[5] What this means is that a library patron who is looking for information on "foreign relations with China" might miss items indexed under UNITED STATES—FOREIGN RELATIONS—CHINA because in the conventional library catalog, the user probably would not think to look under United States for materials about China. Although this is a serious problem, it can in part be overcome by assiduous use of the Library of Congress Subject Headings and a helpful (and knowledgeable!) reference librarian.

The second major problem is that, although cataloging departments do the best they can to assign the appropriate entry points for a library's collection, procedures, terminology and user needs change over time. It is asking too much to expect that subject headings and other entries assigned today will meet the needs of all users in the future.

The Online Approach: Post-coordinated Retrieval

What is required then is the ability to do *post-coordinated retrieval*. This term means that at the time a user needs the information, he can construct a set of entry points to the catalog that will identify a set of items of interest. Further, the user should not be constrained by the limitations of existing entries that were assigned in the past. Not being constrained by existing entries implies keyword access to the entire bibliographic citation and the use of Boolean operators to assist in the retrieval function.

In an operational sense, post-coordinated retrieval means that the library user can put together a set of specifications that describes the type of information being sought. For example, a patron might want poetry by Robert Frost about New Hampshire. In the conventional library catalog, the user would be pretty much left with the prospect of spending a morning browsing through the Robert Frost drawer in the catalog or asking a reference librarian. But the online catalog (if properly implemented) can make this type of search relatively easy to do.

The key phrase here is "if properly implemented." As noted previously, an online catalog is not merely a transposition of the conventional catalog to the computer. An online catalog (at a minimum) must provide keyword access to the entire bibliographic citation and must provide Boolean operators so that the user can perform the desired post-coordinated retrieval functions.

Importance of Boolean Operators

The most common Boolean operators used for online retrieval are AND, OR and NOT. A brief explanation of their use is given in Figure 1.1.

---

5. John R. Sharp, *Some Fundamentals of Information Retrieval* (New York: London House and Maxwell, 1965), p.78.

Figure 1.1: Explanation of Boolean Operators

Example 1: The Library's Holdings

Consider the large rectangle in Example 1 to be the set of all bibliographic citations describing the library's holdings. Now, consider a subset of those holdings that are all the works written by Robert Frost.

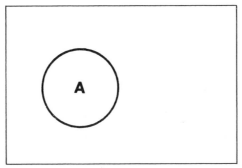

Let set A = the works of Robert Frost

Example 2: The Subset of the Library's Holdings
Written by Robert Frost

Next, consider another subset of the library's holdings, namely, all the works that are poetry.

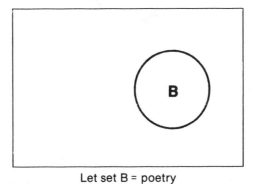

Let set B = poetry

Example 3: The Subset of the Library's Holdings that Is Poetry

Then the intersection of these two sets, that is, poetry by Robert Frost is expressed by the Boolean expression

A AND B.

Figure continues

Figure 1.1: Explanation of Boolean Operators (cont.)

Example 4 shows a schematic representation of this operation.

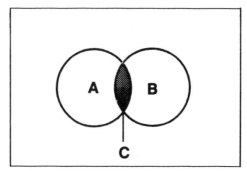

Let set C = poetry by Robert Frost or C = A AND B

Example 4: Venn Diagram Showing the Boolean AND Operator

The Boolean operator OR is used when more than one identifier is needed to describe the information being sought, for example, "poetry by Robert Frost or Robert Burns." The Boolean expression for this is constructed as follows:

Let set A = poetry

Let set B = Robert Frost

Let set C = Robert Burns

Example 5 shows a schematic representation of the Boolean OR operator.

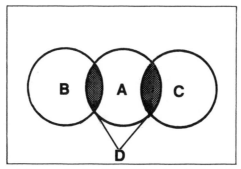

Let set D = poetry by Robert Frost or Robert Burns

Set D = A AND (B OR C)

Example 5: Venn Diagram Showing the Boolean OR Operator

The Boolean operator NOT is used when it is easier to describe what is not wanted than what is. For example, works by Robert Frost that are not poetry might include letters, essays, addresses and so forth. This set of items is difficult to describe except as being "not poetry." Thus, the Boolean operator NOT can be used to describe this set as shown below.

Let set A = works by Robert Frost

Let set B = poetry

Let set C = works by Robert Frost that are not poetry

Figure 1.1: Explanation of Boolean Operators (cont.)

The Boolean expression is A BUT NOT B.

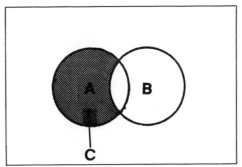

Let set C = works by Robert Frost that are not poetry

Example 6: Venn Diagram Showing the Boolean NOT Operator

It is easy to see what a powerful retrieval tool this is and why we say that the online catalog must provide these capabilities at the very least. There are other features that can add to the effectiveness of the online catalog, but the basic underlying difference between the online catalog and the conventional library catalog is the ability to perform post-coordinated retrieval. No system that does not provide this crucial feature can truly be called an online catalog. At the very least, an online catalog must provide post-coordinated retrieval for the author, title and subject fields in a bibliographic citation. Keyword access to these and other fields is a highly desirable extension.

Keyword Access

Keyword access means that individual words within names, titles, subject headings and other parts of the bibliographic citation may be searched as individual entities. Thus, a library user can look for the name "Xavier" or "Amadeus" and retrieve citations where those words appear in any part of the name fields. It also ensures that the user looking for information on "foreign relations with China" can retrieve those items that are indexed under UNITED STATES—FOREIGN RELATIONS—CHINA. Keyword access provides in-depth retrieval over the entire bibliographic record. When combined with the capacity to perform Boolean operations, a truly powerful retrieval tool results.

Phrase Searching

There may be instances, however, when a library user wants to find only those items that are indicated by a certain heading. In this particular case, the keyword approach may retrieve more items than are wanted, yielding a retrieval set that has relatively low precision. In order to provide this more restrictive retrieval capability, an online catalog can also be searched on entire entries such as author names or subject headings. This is generally known as *phrase searching*. This feature is extremely useful to patrons who are very familiar with the existing library catalog and already know how to find the information they want.

Right-hand Truncation

While some online catalogs provide only phrase searching, many now perform implicit right-hand truncation. Here, the user need only enter as much of the beginning of the phrase as is known. The system then expands the scope of the search to include all the variants that begin with the characters entered by the user. For example, a search on SMITH in such a system might retrieve items indexed under the following headings:

> SMITH
> SMITH, ADAM
> SMITH, JOHN
> SMITH, RUPERT
> SMITHSON, JAMES
> SMITHSONIAN INSTITUTION

The user then can select the appropriate one (or ones) and continue the search.

Authority Control in the Card Catalog

The conventional library catalog is created under authority control. The form of the name and other entries is prescribed by the appropriate set of cataloging rules, and there are guidelines for the assignment of subject headings. Most cataloging systems depend on voluntary compliance with these rules and guidelines to keep the catalog under authority control. This means that although everyone tries to follow the rules and guidelines in the same way and enter the various headings in the correct form, there is no computer-based validation of the headings. True authority control requires that no bibliographic citation be added to the catalog without each entry or heading being validated against some master authority file. This is a very expensive task. Therefore, most systems do not perform machine-validation of headings except to ensure that certain mandatory fields are present.

Authority Control in the Online Catalog

The online catalog may be created in much the same way. In fact, most online catalog data bases were created by using the bibliographic citations produced as a byproduct from the generation of machine-readable catalog cards. Thus, the data in a conventional library catalog and an online catalog may be identical—the difference (as already noted) is in how the data are accessed. The bibliographic records in most online catalogs were created using the same voluntary compliance approach to validation and authority control as the card catalog. The result is that there are numerous inconsistencies and errors in the online catalog data base as well.

These minor inconsistencies in the data can cause retrieval problems because the computer has no way of knowing that ELIOT, THOMAS STEARNS and ELIOT, THOMAS STEARNS, 1885-1965 are variant forms of the same name. Although these and similar inconsistencies in the data bases may cause some difficulties in online use at the outset, they nevertheless are much easier to correct in the online catalog than they were in the earlier system. Thus, careful review and editing of the online data base will gradually eliminate them and the result will be a data base with the internal consistency that was the goal of authority control in the first place.

Authority Cross-references

Authority cross-references are another matter. In the conventional library catalog, these are used to lead the patron from unauthorized to authorized forms of names and other headings and to show related names and concepts. The question of whether to implement this feature in an online catalog is unresolved. Many existing online catalog systems do not now provide this feature although many librarians have indicated that it is almost mandatory.

The difficulty comes in how to implement it. There are several options:

1. Allow the user to browse in an authority file that is maintained separately from the online catalog data base and select the appropriate terminology from this list;

2. Have the system display cross-reference information to the user whenever the user enters a heading or term for which cross-reference information exists; and

3. Develop a large entry vocabulary and a set of mappings to the authorized terminology so that whenever an unauthorized term is entered, it is automatically translated to the correct form.

All of these options have been tried in one or more systems, and there is as yet no clear indication of the best method. It may turn out that the nature of the online catalog data base, its particular group of users and its anticipated use may dictate the choice.

Of course, before turning its attention to catalog design, a library must first address the question of whether an online catalog is appropriate. The next chapter examines some of the issues that may affect the library's decision.

2

Determining the Need for an Online Catalog

As defined and described in Chapter 1, a properly designed online catalog is a powerful tool. But the online catalog is not appropriate for every library. This chapter will examine the issues that libraries must consider before deciding whether to automate the catalog.

ADVANTAGES AND DISADVANTAGES

First, the library should be aware of both the advantages and disadvantages of the online catalog.

Advantages

A primary advantage is that the online catalog data base can be searched on virtually any item of information of interest to the user. Thus, searches such as the following will be relatively easy to perform:

- John Irving's newest book (I don't know the title).

- Any work with a critique or analysis of Shakespeare's "Hamlet."

- Any information on the "Law of the Sea."

- Any works in the library published before 1650.

- An edition of "Grimm's Fairy Tales" with illustrations by Arthur Rackham.

- Essays or addresses by Robert Frost.

- A recent book on Japanese-American trade relations, but in English.

- A first edition with illustrations by N.C. Wyeth.

- A bibliography on air pollution.

- Recent publications of the Elm Tree Press.

These illustrations show the versatility and power of the online catalog. Notice that it is a far different product from the typical conventional library catalog, and the user—either librarian or patron—can get far more information from it. The other advantages of the online catalog may be summarized as follows:

- Library users can retrieve information from the catalog in a variety of ways that were not specified during creation of the catalog. Retrieval criteria can be changed at any time to meet user needs without changing the online catalog data base.

- Global changes can be made easily; that is, if a change in library practice decrees that the form of catalog entries shall be different, the change can be made throughout the entire data base virtually instantaneously. The classic example is moving all the items that have been entered under CLEMENS, SAMUEL LANGHORNE to TWAIN, MARK.

- Filing is no longer a consideration, since items in the catalog do not have to be located according to various filing rules. The internal logic of the online catalog system can retrieve like groups of citations and arrange them logically with each other in any order specified by the user. Thus, the same set of citations might be arranged by call number, by author, by title, by publication date or almost any other field desired.

- The online catalog provides very rapid search capabilities. For a single title known item search—e.g., John Gardner's *October Light*—it may be faster to conduct the search in the card catalog, but for almost any other (even slightly more complex) search, the computer will almost certainly be quicker.

- The online catalog data base can be updated online or at frequent intervals, as desired. Delays resulting from the slow process of filing catalog cards will be eliminated. Further, citations for items that are on order can also appear in the catalog before the catalog cards for them would normally have been produced.

- The online catalog can be used from locations other than the library and at times when the library is closed. This increased access expands the availability of the libraries' collections tremendously.

- The online catalog may save some money. The costs of maintaining an online catalog may actually be slightly less than maintaining its manual counterpart. (Costs are discussed more fully in Chapter 5.)

Disadvantages

Despite its many virtues, the online catalog does have some disadvantages compared to the card catalog.

• The online catalog search logic is more sensitive to minor variations in spelling than the human eye. For example, if you were looking in the card catalog for ELIOT, THOMAS STEARNS, and came across a card with the entry ELIOT, THOMAS STERNS, you would quickly realize that the entries are the same and that the second merely contains a small mistake. The computer—poor, dumb, literal beast that it is—would not be able to equate the two and would not retrieve the citation with the error. On the other hand, because it is relatively easy to correct errors in the online catalog, these inconsistencies gradually can be eliminated. This would be a virtually impossible task in the card catalog, but can be achieved in time with the online version.

• The online catalog requires a new way of getting information. Some well-established techniques that work in the card catalog may not be as successful in the online catalog and the results are likely to be different. For example, many experienced conventional catalog users may begin a search by looking for a known item. The citation for this item will then indicate some subject headings that might lead to other materials of interest. Depending on the online catalog, the results of this subject search (if it can be done at all) may be quite different from a similar search in the card catalog.

• The user may be frustrated by getting too few citations. When using the card catalog, if a user looks under a particular heading and finds no entries, his next step is usually to consult a librarian to find out what the correct heading is or where the desired information may be found. With the online catalog, there is a tendency to believe the computer response—no matter how ludicrous.

• The user may also occasionally get too many citations—say 10,000. In the card catalog, the normal response to two drawers of Shakespeare cards is to think of another way to look for the desired information. The same approach will work in the online catalog, but users do not always think about how to make a search more precise.

• The computer can occasionally retrieve what are known as *false drops*. These are citations that are retrieved in response to a particular search request but which are not relevant to the topic in question. The classic example is the word WOOD, which might retrieve books about wood and also books by an author named Wood. Although this sounds as if it might be a serious problem, in actual practice it has turned out to be more of a source of amusement than a significant problem for users.

• The online catalog can be unavailable if there is a power failure or if the computer breaks down. The likelihood of these things happening and the availability of fail-safe procedures makes the prospect less calamitous than it was in the past. Nevertheless, it remains a major concern of libraries and therefore one of the major disadvantages of an online catalog. With all its shortcomings, the card catalog is always "up," and if there is light enough to see, people can use it.

THE ONLINE CATALOG: FACTORS TO CONSIDER

Let us now examine some of the factors that determine whether a library should consider installing an online catalog. Although the factors will vary somewhat according to individual circumstances, there are a few general guidelines that can be laid down. These involve the size of the collection, the needs of the library patrons and staff, the size and demographics of the user population, whether the library has converted some of its citations to machine-readable form and cost.

Size of the Collection

Small and Medium-sized Collections

A question frequently asked by libraries contemplating online catalogs is: "How small is too small?" The answer varies somewhat according to the nature of the collection and user needs, but in general, a collection of up to 10,000 titles can be handled very nicely with a card or other manual catalog. This is because the collection is small enough so that the librarian and the users will quickly become acquainted with the collection. Browsing will serve very well to locate items in the collection. In fact, except as an inventory management device, the library may not need a catalog at all.

A collection of up to 100,000 items is still manageable by traditional techniques, but is too large for most people to know completely. Therefore, online access to the citations will be useful in locating materials that might be otherwise "lost" because of cataloging inconsistencies, inadequate subject headings and other shortcomings of the traditional catalog. Filing problems may start to become evident in a collection of this size. If the user population is large and diverse, an online catalog (and almost certainly, an online circulation system) will be a necessity.

Large Collections

A collection of half a million titles or so almost certainly would justify the expense of an online catalog. With a collection of this size, card catalog maintenance costs are considerable. As the collection increases in size, the cost/benefit of an online catalog becomes greater. With large collections, however, the cost of retrospective conversion becomes a major consideration. A library may have to make a decision to close the existing catalog as of a certain date and continue with an online catalog for all new materials. Considering that the use of most library materials falls off very rapidly with age, in a very few years the online catalog should be meeting the needs of most of its users—even though it includes only a part of the collection.

Finally, there is the question of the very large library with millions of titles and thousands of users. Unquestionably, an online catalog would assist the retrieval problems posed by these enormous collections, but it is still stretching the state of the art to provide this kind of online catalog at a cost that is not prohibitive. As online storage and processing costs continue to decline, it may be possible to put these catalogs online as well. Today, only a few large government libraries, such as the Library of Congress or the National Library of Medicine, and a few others such as the University of California system, can afford this option.

Determining the Needs of Library Users

At a recent workshop on training users of online catalogs, it became obvious that there were wide differences among the various online catalogs being demonstrated and described.[1] It gradually became apparent that at least some of the differences were attributable to the varying needs of library users.

The easiest online patron access catalogs to use are probably the ones with touch panels such as those marketed by CL Systems, Inc. (CLSI) and DataPhase Systems, Inc. In at least one CLSI installation, where there is a relatively high number of semi-literate library users, the alphabet is posted on the side of the terminal. It is useful for children and those of us who just can't always remember whether "U" comes before "V" or after "W."

Some online catalogs intended for use in public library settings have very friendly user dialogs and procedures. Other systems, often found in academic libraries or other settings in which there is a more or less captive audience, use far more complex procedures because their patrons can be required to participate in library orientation programs and training sessions.

At the heart of all this is that a library considering installing an online catalog must consider the needs of its patrons above everything else. Staff needs, of course, must be taken into account, but the underlying design philosophy must regard the online catalog primarily as a tool for the library's users. If the online catalog is also to serve some other functions (as it would in an integrated library system, discussed in Chapter 8) these other requirements must be considered. But the most important requirement is still to satisfy the needs of the library patrons.

B.L. Krieger, Dartmouth Library

<hr>

1. Conference on Training Users of Online Catalogs, Council on Library Resources and Trinity University, San Antonio, TX, January 12-14, 1983.

Some of the questions that the library will need to ask are:

• Are the library's users willing to learn to use an online catalog?

• Does the library have many one-time users or many infrequent users who might not remember from one time to the next how to use the online catalog?

• What are the demographics of the user population? Are there large numbers of children or elderly people who use the library? (This might influence the library's choice of catalog; e.g., it might put in a touch-panel system.)

• What is the general literacy level? Computer literacy level?

• What sort of information needs are characteristic of the user group? Are there a few types that predominate? (For example, an online catalog with brief records meets public library needs, but is insufficient for most academic library needs.)

• Would the users benefit from being able to query the library's catalog from locations outside the library?

• What is the estimated volume of catalog inquiries per year? (Very few inquiries would indicate that an online catalog is not needed, even if the collection is large.)

The Online Catalog Data Base

Whether the library has any of its catalog in machine-readable form is a critical factor in deciding to install an online catalog. In Chapter 3, we will discuss some aspects of creating a data base for the online catalog. We need only note here that the library that has (wisely!) been doing its cataloging in machine-readable form for some years and has a sizeable portion of its catalog in that form is way ahead of the game. Retrospective conversion is expensive and time-consuming, thus, the library that has planned for eventual automation has a great advantage.

Cost

Finally, the library will need to ask how much it is spending on maintaining the existing catalog and if it can manage to pay the cost of an online catalog. Chapter 5 will discuss these issues in more detail, but for general planning purposes, the library should keep the following in mind:

• Installing an online catalog will probably not eliminate any jobs—some of the tasks that library staff members do may change, but just as many man-hours will be needed.

• Computer equipment continues to get less and less expensive while labor costs rise. There will probably come a time when converting to an online catalog, while not saving much money, will keep the costs from rising any faster.

• The start-up cost is only the beginning. Although the amount needed to purchase a system is often large, it is a one-time cost that may be covered in a variety of ways. Once over that hurdle, the library will have to plan for the continuing costs that the online catalog will entail. Keep in mind that these costs may in fact be less than the cost of the card catalog; however, they will involve different budget items.

SUMMARY

The decision to install an online catalog will depend heavily on a library's particular circumstances. The proliferation of online catalog systems coming on the market now is but one indication that no single system can meet the needs of all libraries. A library can ensure that it makes the right decisions about whether to install an online catalog (and if so, which one) by a careful and thorough analysis of its needs. A review of the CONDOC specifications (described in Chapter 1) may be helpful, but the library must compile its own list of requirements.

In order to accomplish this vital task, the library will probably need to appoint yet another committee or task force to review the information and prepare a recommendation. The committee should comprise no more than six members. It should include at least two users, a representative from public services, a representative from technical services and someone with knowledge of library automation, costs, budgeting, grants and contracts.

The result of the committee's work should be a list of *requirements* (a list of problems to be solved) rather than a list of *specifications* (what the system is to do). Let the systems designers decide how best to meet the library's requirements. Only the library can define what its needs are. If needs can be stated clearly, solutions can be proposed. Then, in reviewing the various alternatives, the library can select the ones that best meet its needs. The other approach—listing specifications—limits the range of solutions to what has been specified already, when there may be other alternatives that meet the library's needs better.

If the recommendation is that the library does need an online catalog, the committee should focus on how library patrons will want to use the new system. Once this is done, the library will be able to see if any of the available systems meets its needs and make a wise choice among the offerings. Available systems will be described in Chapter 6. Chapter 3 will discuss the structure of the online data base.

3

Creating the Data Base

Although the features of the online catalog system are important to its success, the content and form of the online catalog data base are crucial. There are several aspects to consider:

- What library materials will be included in the online catalog;

- What bibliographic information will be available in the online catalog;

- How this information will be stored and accessed;

- Retrospective conversion; and

- Future extensions.

This chapter will present some thoughts on each of these topics and will provide some guidelines for libraries that are trying to build an online catalog data base.

MATERIALS TO BE INCLUDED

What materials should be included in the online catalog? The simple answer to this question is "everything," and ultimately, that will no doubt be the case. In the short run, however, there are some limitations.

Limitations of Cataloging Formats

For example, the bibliographic utilities, notably the Online Computer Library Center (OCLC) and the Research Libraries Group (RLG), provide cataloging formats for many but not all types of materials. Originally, only cataloging of monographic materials was possible. Today, serials, maps, music, audiovisuals and manuscript materials may be cataloged using these systems. Thus, a library now can create machine-readable records for almost all types of materials in its collections. However, there are still library materials that cannot be cataloged: magnetic tapes and discs, computer software and other forms of new media.

In addition, materials that are in non-Roman alphabets are difficult to catalog appropriately. New terminals and software are gradually being developed which will accommodate Cyrillic, Hebrew, Asian and other non-Roman character sets, but for the time being the only practical method of adding these items to the online catalog is to transliterate or translate the bibliographic information.

A further problem arises for those languages that use the Roman alphabet but have diacritics and other special characters. These characters are not usually available on standard terminal keyboards and screen displays. Other important aspects of this problem will be considered later in this chapter in the discussion of how data are stored and accessed in the online catalog.

User Preferences

A 1982 Council of Library Resources study revealed that many online catalog users wanted more materials to be included in the catalog. In cases where periodical titles, newspapers, government documents or other large classes of materials were not included, users clearly indicated that they wanted these items added to the data base. Further, users said that they wanted the library's older materials included as well. (The Council study will be discussed in detail in Chapter 7.)

In short, users would like to have one place (the online catalog) in which to look for items of interest. If they do not locate the desired materials there, they know that further searching is pointless: the library does not have the material. Conversely, they know that if they conduct a successful search in which a great deal of relevant material is retrieved, it is likely that they have found all or most of the material that the library holds.

Different Collections

Many libraries that have several branches or several sub-collections (such as manuscripts, maps, music) may have special catalogs for these materials. In the past, library users may have had to consult several separate card catalogs in order to be sure they had covered all of the library's holdings. The online catalog, if it is comprehensive, can provide an enormous service to users by making these different collections available in one place. This factor is also a strong argument in favor of retrospective conversion (converting bibliographic information to machine-readable form). Once the information has been converted, the records can be used for the online catalog or for any other library application.

The Shared Catalog

In addition to providing as complete coverage as possible for its own holdings, a library can include its data base in a union catalog or regional cooperative online data base. This pooled or shared online catalog makes the collections of each participating library available to the others for interlibrary loan and other cooperative programs.

BIBLIOGRAPHIC CITATIONS

Controversy rages over the format and type of bibliographic information that should be included in the online catalog. The alternatives range from including the entire MARC record, with all the subfields and the entire tagging structure, to a highly abbreviated record which may include only the call number, author and title. The reasons for this disparity are partly historical and partly because there is no agreement on what an online catalog is and what its function should be.

Form of the Citation

Historically, a number of online catalogs developed as outgrowths of systems that had originally been designed for another purpose. The classic example of this is the online catalog that began as a circulation system. Another is the online catalog that is an outgrowth of an online cataloging system such as OCLC and the Research Libraries Information Network (RLIN).

Brief Records

The online circulation systems generally did not pretend to be online catalogs and their bibliographic citations were brief records, sufficient to identify the item. These records in no way claimed to replace the bibliographic information contained in the card or other manual catalog, and the circulation system was intended to be used in conjunction with the library card or other catalog. Figure 3.1 shows a sample record from a CL Systems, Inc. (CLSI) circulation system data base.

Full MARC Records

The online cataloging systems such as OCLC and RLIN were designed to provide library staff with a tool to be used in processing library materials. These systems use as the bibliographic record the full MARC format with all the tags, subfield codes and other indicators. This level of detail is essential for cataloging work but may provide more information than most online catalog users need. Figure 3.2 illustrates a typical MARC record from OCLC, and Figure 3.3 shows a typical RLIN record.

Content of the Citation

Studies at Dartmouth College and the University of Guelph show that most catalog users do not need the entire bibliographic record when consulting the catalog.[1] Users tell us that they want improved access to information contained in the table of contents, summary

---

1. E.J. Lindsay, "Familiarity, Use, and Importance of Information on Library Catalog Cards," Technical Report No. 9 (Hanover, NH: Dartmouth College, September 25, 1978).

Figure 3.1: Sample Bibliographic Record from an Online Circulation System

```
Book 1:    AZ 105.B6
Title:     Computers in humanistic research;    readings and ...
Author:    Bowles, Edmind A     comp.


Book 2:    AZ 111.06
Title:     Computers and the humanities
Author:    City University of New York.    Queen's College.


Book 3:    AC   5.R33 v.41  no. 6
Title:     Computers and society,    edited by George A. Nikolaieff
Author:    Nikolaieff, George A     comp.
```

Figure 3.2: Sample OCLC Record

```
NO HOLDINGS IN DRB -  FOR HOLDINGS ENTER dh DEPRESS  DISPLAY RECD SEN

OCLC: 1200309      Rec stat: c Entrd: 750305        Used: 830613
Type: a Bib lvl: m Govt pub:   Lang:  eng Source:   Illus: f
Repr:    Enc lvl: I Conf pub: 0 Ctry: nyu Dat tp: s M/F/B: 11
Indx: 0 Mod rec: m Festschr: 0 Cont:
Desc:   Int lvl:   Dates: 1903,
  1 010      03-29612
  2 040      DLC c KSU d m.c. d SER
  3 041 0    engfre
  4 050 0    PZ3.C59 b Ju
  5 049      DRBB
  6 100 10   Twain, Mark, d 1835-1910. w cn
  7 245 14   The Jumping frog, b in English, then in French, then clawed back
into a civilized language once more by patient, unremunerated toil, c by Mark
Twain [pseud.] illustrated by F. Strothman.
  8 260 0    New York, a London, b Harper & Brothers, c 1903.
  9 300      2 p. >., 65, [1] p. b front., 11 pl. c 21 cm.
 10 870 19   j 100/1 a [Clemens, Samuel Langhorne] d 1835-1910.
```

Figure 3.3: Sample RLIN Records

```
  PROD      BOOKS       PRI       MIUG83-B39611          SEARCH          NHDG-OID
CLUSTER 1 OF 290
+B
HEMINGWAY, ERNEST.
   GOD REST YOU MERRY GENTLEMEN. NEW YORK : HOUSE OF BOOKS, 1933.
   ONE OF 300 COPIES.

   ID: MIUG83-B39611              CC: 9668      DCF: ?
- - - - - - - - - - - - - - - - - - - - - - - - - - - - - - - - - - -
MIUG (A-9668 MIU)
¦
```

Short form

```
  PROD      BOOKS      FUL/BIB  MIUG83-B39611          SEARCH          NHDG-OID
CLUSTER 1 OF 290
+B
ID:MIUG83-B39611    RTYP:A    ST:P   FRN:    NLR:      MS:  EL:  AD:06-03-83
CC:9668   BLT:AM    DCF:?   CSC:?   MOD:?   SNR:      ATC:      UD:06-03-83
CP:NYU    L:ENG     INT:?   GPC:?   BIO:?   FIC:?   CON:????
PC:S      PD:1933/          REP:?   CPI:?   FSI:?   ILC:????  MEI:?   II:?
100 10  HEMINGWAY, ERNEST.
245 10  GOD REST YOU MERRY GENTLEMEN.
260 0   NEW YORK :‡BHOUSE OF BOOKS,‡C1933.
300     ONE OF 300 COPIES.
X
```

Long form

and indexes of items in the collection. For the most part, however, they do not need to see the collation, imprint, series statements and other parts of the record in order to decide if an item is of interest to them. These findings argue for the following compromise: include the entire bibliographic record in the data base and enhance it (if possible) with table of contents and index information, but display only a brief form of the record to online catalog users.

B.L. Krieger, Dartmouth Library

Whether to retain the MARC tagging structure in the bibliographic citation depends on how the online catalog is to be used—as a cataloging tool or solely as a reference source. Controlled searches using the textual information contained in the bibliographic records and the MARC fixed fields yielded consistently better results when the text information was searched. This is because the fixed fields came into use at different times and have not been consistently applied in the cataloging process. Thus, while it is true that use of the MARC fixed fields and tags may lead to greater precision in search results, if these fields and tags were incorrectly or inconsistently applied, relevant materials may also be missed.

Of course, one answer to this problem is to "clean up the data base," but this seems to be an extremely costly and generally hopeless task. If cataloging practice could be frozen now and for all time, it might be possible to correct all the errors in the online catalog data base once and for all and go on to build a perfect product. But this is not likely to happen. Hardly had *AACR2* settled into place when there were rumors of *AACR3*, and modifications to the MARC format are continually being proposed.

Thus, a much better solution for the long term is to design the online catalog to overcome the problems of inconsistencies in the data base. This is yet another argument in favor of free-text searching of the entire bibliographic record, because no matter what changes are made in the future or what inconsistencies remain from the past, the data are still accessible in a more versatile fashion.

Storing and Accessing the Data

As noted earlier, there are problems with actually storing the text of some bibliographic citations in the online catalog data base. These involve citations that are in non-Roman alphabets or that have diacritics and other special characters. Basically, there are three alternatives for storing diacritics in the online data base.

1. Place the diacritic immediately following the character it is used with. This only works if the system can display all the special characters; e.g., Ko:nig.

2. Transliterate the character plus diacritic combination to its equivalent; e.g., König becomes Koenig.

3. Take them all out.

The first alternative looks very strange in the bibliographic citation and certainly would not be the way a patron enters search words. The second option looks fine, but the user must know what the transliterations are, and there can be conflicts between the language of the item and the language of the term being transliterated. The third alternative, while it makes purists unhappy, is the only realistic one for today's online catalogs, given the limitations of terminals and software.

A similar problem arises with mathematical, chemical and other technical works that use special symbols. The only good solution to this problem is to avoid it; that is, to use titles and other bibliographic information that describe the item in ordinary text.

In the future, when terminals, printers and software are available that can handle non-Roman character sets, the library will undoubtedly want to reload the data base with these special characters. In the meantime, most users can get along without them.

DATA BASE DESIGN TECHNIQUES

Library applications have historically stretched the capabilities of computer systems. The record formats are more complex and the data base sizes are much larger than more conventional computer applications. A typical MARC record with all the tags and subfield indicators contains about 750 characters. Thus, a library collection of only 100,000 items will require 75 million bytes of online storage just to house the bibliographic records.

Until quite recently, the cost of storing these quantities of data was prohibitive for all but large government organizations (such as the National Library of Medicine) and large regional or nationwide networks or services. Further, the high cost of online storage dictated in some instances how the online catalog data should be stored. In essence, any techniques that could be used to minimize the amount of online storage needed were advantageous because they brought the cost down.

Several of the online catalog systems that were developed in the early 1970s reflect this philosophy. Examples are CL Systems, Inc. (CLSI) and Northwestern's NOTIS system. To their credit, each is an operational online catalog system that, at the time it was developed, was stretching the state of the art. Since that time, the cost of online storage has come down dramatically. In addition, systems designers have learned how to compress text files and build much more efficient data structures and search procedures. Therefore, it is now possible to create online catalog files and to provide highly sophisticated search access to them even on microcomputers, and at very low cost.

There is now no reason why online catalogs should not have free-text searching and use of Boolean operators. Data base design techniques can provide these features at a reasonable cost both for storage and computer processing time. Librarians should ask for these features and expect to find them in the online catalogs being developed today.

Inverted File

Although the data base structures needed to provide these capabilities are implemented in different ways, the basic technique is to create what is know as an *inverted file*. Inverted files are of two types: the "pure" inverted file and the inverted index or directory. A pure inverted file organizes the data so that logically the bibliographic records are stored in a block following whatever heading is selected for them. For example, the author name "Eliot, Thomas Stearns 1865- " might be the heading for a group of bibliographic citations for which Eliot is the author. Logically, these would be stored as illustrated in Figure 3.4.

Figure 3.4: A Pure Inverted File Structure

Eliot, Thomas Stearns 1865-	Record 1	Record 2	⟶	Record N*

*N: Any number

It is easy to see that this type of structure provides a quick and easy way to perform author searches, especially where the authorized form of the name is known. Further, it is easy to implement right-hand truncation with this scheme because the system merely looks for all the headings that match whatever the user has entered. Thus, a search on "Eliot T" would retrieve items by "Eliot, T.S." as well as those by "Eliot, Thomas Stearns 1865- ." The technique will also work for title or subject searches. The difficulty arises if free-text searching is desired or if Boolean operators would be helpful, as in author/title searches or compound subject searches.

Inverted Index or Directory

The file structure for inverted index or directory is the same. This technique builds an index for each heading selected that indicates, by means of an identification number (ID number), which items in the data base contain the heading. The index may be further refined to show what part of the record contains the heading or even what position in the text the heading occupies. There is a separate index that shows where each of the bibliographic records is located in the data base. Figure 3.5 shows a schematic representation of an inverted index.

This method of organizing the online catalog data base requires more data storage space and more processing time. However, it can easily provide free-text searching over the entire bibliographic data base. Boolean operators can be implemented, and, while their use certainly entails more computer processing, the additional retrieval power they provide is well worth it.

Figure 3.5: An Inverted Index or Directory File Structure

Eliot
ID Number for Record 1
ID Number for Record 2
ID Number for Record N*

ID Number for Record 1	Location
ID Number for Record 2	Location
ID Number for Record N	Location

N: Any Number

In addition, with a little more programming, this file structure can be made to provide the same sort of right-hand truncation as the pure inverted file structure. Adding this capability requires *double posting* certain fields such as author names and subject terms. Double posting means that not only is each individual word in the citation included in the inverted index, but there are entries for the full name and heading entries as well. Of course, these techniques require more storage, but as we have already noted, the cost of online storage is steadily decreasing.

RETROSPECTIVE CONVERSION

As mentioned earlier, it is important to have as much of the library's collection included in the online data base as possible. Most libraries will have some but not all of their citations in machine-readable form. A few very new libraries may be able to do all their cataloging in machine-readable form from the beginning, and thus build an online data base which is truly representative of the library's collection.

Older libraries are not so fortunate. Some have only a few thousand titles in machine-readable form, with hundreds of thousands of unconverted records. What to do about the remainder is the problem. The choices are:

● Forget about the older materials. Freeze the card catalog and continue to build an online catalog for the new materials.

● Create machine-readable records for all items and add them to the online data base.

● Get machine-readable records for as many items as possible and forget about the rest.

Libraries will have to choose for themselves which of these options is the most appropriate. The choice will depend on the size of the collection, the percentage of records in machine-readable form, the patrons' needs for older materials and the costs of doing retrospective conversion. Assuming that a library decides to do some retrospective conversion, there are again several alternatives:

● Use one of the bibliographic utilities such as OCLC, RLG, the Washington Library Network (WLN), or a service such as Carrollton Press, to obtain machine-readable records for older materials. This is probably the best method of getting high-quality records for older materials.

● Contract with one of the keyboarding services to convert the library's shelflist. This would be a good alternative for a corporate or other special library which has a high percentage of materials that are unique to that library and are not likely to be included in any other data base.

● Recatalog the older materials. This may be required if they were originally cataloged using another system (e.g., Dewey versus Library of Congress) and if it is desirable to make the entire collection consistent throughout. The major disadvantage of this option is that it is extremely expensive.*

FUTURE EXTENSIONS

One of the major conclusions of the Council on Library Resources patron access study is that users would like to have enhanced subject access to bibliographic materials. This could be achieved by enriching the bibliographic citations to include tables of contents and index information.

Another possibility would be to include abstracts of materials in the collection. Then users who find titles of items that look promising could view the abstracts and decide if the item is likely to be of value.

Making either of these changes would require adding new fields to the MARC format and providing guidelines for how the additional information is to be entered. The cost of cataloging would increase, because providing these extensions would require more time for each item being processed, but the benefit to users is almost certainly worth it.

---

*For a discussion of data conversion in libraries, see Ruth C. Carter and Scott Bruntjen, *Data Conversion* (White Plains, NY: Knowledge Industry Publications, Inc., 1983); and Susan Baerg Epstein, "Converting Bibliographic Records for Automation," *Library Journal* 108(5) (March 1, 1983): 474-76 and "Converting Records for Automation at the Copy Level," *Library Journal* 108(7) (April 1, 1983): 642-43.

4

Installing an Online Catalog:
Moving from Theory to Practice

In the preceding chapters, we have discussed online catalogs in relatively abstract terms. This chapter will review some of the factors involved in actually installing an online catalog. To automate the catalog (or, for that matter, almost any other library function) a library must provide several things:

- A machine-readable data base of cataloging records and the means for updating it;

- Access to a computer;

- System software;

- Terminals for library patrons and staff;

- A way to connect the terminals to the computer;

- A backup plan in case the system fails;

- Orientation and training for users and staff.

THE ONLINE DATA BASE

The online data base and its creation were discussed in Chapter 3. Here, then, we need only remind systems planners that there must be provision to update and/or maintain the data base. This involves three types of operations:

- Adding a record to the data base;

- Removing a record from the data base;

- Changing a record that is already in the data base.

These maintenance activities can take place online, quasi-online or in batch mode.

Online update means performing the entire data base maintenance operation in real time. That is, when a staff member enters a new record or makes a change to an existing one, the change is entered in the system's data base at the same time. With *quasi-online update*, the record can be inspected and altered on the screen (i.e., online), but the actual changes to the data base are made overnight when the system is idle.

Batch mode data base maintenance usually involves a large number of records. Batch mode updates are not done online; a printed copy of the record is inspected, and alterations are made on some type of correction form. Changes to the data base are generally made overnight, and usually make the system unavailable to users while the data base is being modified. Batch mode updates are often performed by libraries that update their online catalogs once a week or once a month using the Online Computer Library Center (OCLC) or Research Libraries Information Network (RLIN) transaction tapes.

Some systems provide all three types of update operations, allowing the library to choose the most appropriate type for the activity being performed. Of course, online update is the most expensive, but if the results must be seen immediately, it is the only choice. Quasi-online update is easier to implement and may be satisfactory for many libraries. It has the advantage of providing slightly better control over changes than online update, but the results usually cannot be checked until the next day. Batch mode update is often more efficient because the different types of maintenance can be grouped; e.g., all the additions, deletions and modifications to existing records can be processed together. Further, the changes can be loaded from a tape or other high-speed data transfer medium rather than being entered by hand or transferred one-by-one in a computer-to-computer transfer.

ACCESS TO A COMPUTER

The second necessary ingredient in installing an online catalog is access to a computer. The equipment itself is generally known as *hardware*, as distinguished from the *software*, or programs, that "tell" the computer what functions to perform. Hardware usually includes the central processing unit (CPU), disk drives and controllers, tape drives, computer console, high-speed printer and possibly other special purpose devices such as card readers. *Microcomputer, minicomputer* and *mainframe* are terms used to indicate the relative power of the computer system. Although the distinctions become harder and harder to make (some of today's microcomputers are more powerful than the mainframes of 20 years ago), cost, CPU size, type of online storage medium and architecture are the major distinguishing features.*

---

*For a discussion of different types of computers in the library environment, see Richard W. Boss, *The Library Manager's Guide to Automation, 2nd Edition* (White Plains, NY: Knowledge Industry Publications, Inc., in press).

The library has several options for providing computer access:

- Use a computer that already belongs to or is reserved for the library;

- Buy or lease a computer;

- Share a computer with several other libraries, or with another organization or group;

- Purchase computer time from a vendor;

- Purchase equipment, software, installation and training services from a vendor. This is referred to as a "turnkey" system.

The best choice among these options is highly dependent on local circumstances and politics and is best judged by the library administration. The relative costs of these options will be discussed in Chapter 5. Often, however, there are other major factors that affect the decision. Some of these are:

- Does the library have a place to put a computer?

- Are extensive renovations required to provide the proper controlled environment for the equipment?

- If a shared computer is contemplated, how far away will it be? How will the library be connected to it?

- If a shared computer is selected, what priority will the library's applications have? Are there other jobs running on the computer which will interfere with the library's operation? Will response time suffer if other users are on the system?

- Does the system have enough capacity to meet the library's needs?

- Who will maintain the system? Does the computer manufacturer have service facilities in the area? What about the terminals? Who will service them?

- Does the library have its own, or access to, support services and/or personnel who can assist with any of these problems?

The turnkey option is almost always the most expensive, but it may be the best choice for a library with little experience in library automation and with few or no knowledgeable systems personnel available. The other options give the library more latitude in designing a custom system, but at the same time require considerable experience and skill.

Mini- and microcomputers are rarely leased. These devices must generally be purchased, although the library may be able to spread the payments over several years. While the cost of purchasing a computer can be very high, the library will have equipment dedicated to its own applications. The library can then set its own priorities for computer support and operate the system accordingly.

Sharing a computer is an excellent option for libraries that are near each other or for libraries that can cooperate with another organization. These cooperative arrangements often provide much better facilities at lower cost than could any one library acting on its own.

SOFTWARE FOR THE ONLINE CATALOG

A vital part of the online catalog is the system software. Software is a catch-all term for all the programs and underlying systems support features that make the computer perform. Some software may be supplied by the computer manufacturer, some may be available from another source and some may be supplied by the online catalog vendor or written by the library itself. These sets of programs, taken as a group, are called *software* because they are not housed in metal cabinets and may not exist in hard-copy form at all. The major components that are needed are:

• Operating system for the computer. This is always required. It may come "free," with the equipment, but usually there is a separate charge for it.

• Data Base Management System (DBMS). Also known as the data base manager, this software component is needed by some, but not all, systems. The Washington Library Network (WLN) system, which uses ADABAS, and the CTI Library Systems Inc. system, which uses Prime INFORMATION, are among the online catalogs that require this software.

• Communications software. Many computer systems require a special set of programs to handle the communications between the central computer and the terminals or other remote devices. IBM-based systems often use CICS for this purpose; other systems require similar packages. Occasionally, the communications link requires a combination of software and hardware; that is, in some cases special programs and a special piece of equipment, such as a circuit board or controller, are needed.

• Applications programs. These are the programs that actually make the system perform as an online catalog. In general, the applications programs control the functions of specific parts of the online catalog, such as online search, citation display, data base update and the user dialog or interface.

• Special purpose programs. Some libraries may need additional software depending on the type of online catalog being installed. Programs might be needed to convert an existing machine-readable data base to the appropriate form, or possibly to connect the library's online catalog with one of the bibliographic utilities. Special programs may also be needed to customize the applications programs described above to meet specific requirements. For example, a special library with a large collection of report literature might need a specialized load program to add the records for these items to the online catalog data base. It might also need a tailor-made user interface.

TYPES OF ONLINE CATALOG SOFTWARE

In general, choosing the best software is the most important decision a library faces in installing an online catalog. There are many options available. A number of vendors and other organizations now offer software with some online catalog features. These offerings generally fall into two main types: 1) online circulation systems with enhancements for online public access and 2) integrated library systems. As these systems evolve, the distinctions get fuzzier and fuzzier, but their origins are usually evident in the way the systems organize the data base and how they operate. Some vendors that supply online catalogs as enhancements to circulation systems are:

- CL Systems, Inc. (CLSI)

- CTI Library Systems, Inc.

- DataPhase Systems, Inc.

- Geac Canada Ltd.

- Ohio State University

- Universal Library Systems

Among the vendors or institutions that developed online catalogs as one component of an integrated library system are:

- National Library of Medicine/National Technical Information Service

- Biblio-Techniques, Inc.

- Data Research Associates

- Northwestern University

These systems will be described in Chapter 6.

Characteristics of Circulation System-derived Catalogs

Although generalizations are always risky, the two types of online catalog systems have some significant differences. The circulation system-derived catalogs generally share the following characteristics:

- The data base is composed of brief records stripped of MARC tags.

- The data base is often organized so that multiple copies of a given title are treated as a single record.

- The dialog and user procedures are exceptionally well thought out and easy to use (i.e., user friendly). There is a minimum of jargon.

• These systems often work best in environments having large user populations and a comparatively small number of catalog records.

• Search access is usually available only by author, title, call number or other specified field. Often, subject access is not provided, and the use of Boolean operators is frequently limited.

Characteristcs of Integrated System-derived Catalogs

Those online catalogs that were developed as part of an integrated library system have other characteristics in common:

• The data base contains full MARC records and is usually able to display the full MARC tagging structure if desired.

• The systems were generally designed by librarians for librarians and thus, patrons may find them slightly more complicated to use than the circulation system-based catalogs.

• The screen displays generally contain more information and often contain data that can best be characterized as "for library use only." That is, there may be codes and other information shown that are not needed by library patrons, but are useful to library staff.

• There may be provision for cross-references and other authority file capabilities.

• Since the online catalog is part of a larger system, it may contain records for items that are on order or in process.

CHOOSING THE BEST SOFTWARE

Understanding a library's particular requirements and evaluating each offering in terms of its ability to meet them is the crucial factor in choosing good software. At a January 1983 workshop on training for online catalogs,[1] several systems were demonstrated and discussed. The most striking thing about the group of systems was how different they all were. The catalogs differed in content, record format, user commands, display options and method of use. They ran on a variety of computers under several operating systems.

For the most part, there were good reasons for these differences. Some were historical; that is, some online catalogs were derived from other older systems and thus bore the signs of their heritage. Others were a result of the varying information needs of the user populations. For example, a patron at the Evanston (IL) Public Library would hardly have the same needs and expectations of an online catalog as would a researcher at the Library of Congress. Thus, it became clear that each catalog was a solution to an individual library's set of needs and environmental factors and, as such, was the "best" for that particular library.

---

1. Conference on Training Users of Online Catalogs, Council on Library Resources and Trinity University, San Antonio, TX, January 12-14, 1983.

Libraries can sometimes work together to select software for their online catalogs. The Consortium to Develop Online Catalogs (CONDOC) is one group that has been working together for several years to develop specifications for an online catalog and to acquire software that will meet its needs (see Chapter 1). A library contemplating installation of an online catalog might want to review the CONDOC specifications to get an idea of what other libraries have deemed essential, but each library will then have to decide for itself what is required for its particular group of users.[2]

Of course, the computer hardware and systems software decisions must really be made together because not all software runs on all hardware. Thus, while it would be nice to choose independently the best option for each, at this time it is generally not possible. Some online catalog software can operate on a range of computer equipment within a family (e.g., IBM 4331, 4341 or Digital Equipment Corp. 11/34, 11/44, 11/70) or may run on two or more different types of equipment (e.g., on Data General and Tandem equipment, or on Data General and DEC equipment). As programming languages and operating systems become more independent of machines, separating the hardware and software decisions may be possible. For the near future, however, the two decisions are inextricably bound up with each other.

Libraries should keep in mind that choosing the right software is a crucial decision. Hardware can be changed relatively easily (although sometimes expensively), but software that doesn't work, doesn't do what the library needs and can't be modified easily is a disaster. There is no recourse except to go to the vendor or other supplier and try to get it fixed. This route can be costly, time-consuming, frustrating and litigious! It generally leads to bad relations between vendors and libraries and is to be avoided at all costs. The best way to escape this pitfall is by astute choice of software. The library can increase its chances of choosing wisely by understanding its requirements and by careful negotiations with the vendor or other online catalog supplier.

TERMINALS FOR THE ONLINE CATALOG

Once the online catalog hardware and software are chosen, the next crucial decision concerns terminals for library users and staff. Terminals are any devices used to link up with the online catalog from many locations. They can be used to send or receive data to or from the computer. Terminals include visual display terminals (VDTs), printers and even, in some cases, microcomputers.

Number of Terminals to Provide

Before choosing the types of terminals to be used, the library must first address the question "How many do we need?" Probably the correct answer is "as many as you can afford." Other possible guidelines might simply be "twice as many as you think you need now" and "more." Studies have shown that users want terminals—lots of terminals—and they want them not only in the library but in other locations. For a public library, this might mean

---

2. Consortium to Develop an Online Catalog (CONDOC), *Specifications for an Online Catalog* (Chicago: November 2, 1981).

placing terminals near the entrance, in the children's room and in the stacks; it might also mean providing dial-up access for patrons who have terminals at home. In an academic setting, this might mean putting terminals in all the libraries, in the stacks, in study areas and ultimately in dormitories and other non-classroom spaces.

Types of Terminals

There are several types of terminals that can be used for an online catalog. These can be grouped into two main classes: those that produce hard-copy (paper) output and those that display information on a screen (soft-copy).

Hard-copy Terminals or Printers

The most common types of printers are:

• Thermal or quiet printer. These operate by burning a spot in specially treated paper. They can be expensive to operate because the paper is not cheap, but they are excellent for use in areas where noise is a consideration. The print quality of thermal printers is generally not letter quality.

• Impact printer. Impact printers come in a wide variety of styles and prices. All make the image on paper by action similar to a typewriter. The two types are daisy wheel, which are letter quality printers, and dot matrix, which are not.

• High-speed printer. These printers are attached directly to the computer or there may be one or more remote printers to serve several users. High-speed printers are widely used to print lengthy bibliographies and other large files of textual information. The print is generally not letter quality.

• Laser printer. These devices are very high-speed printers, used for rapid printing of very large files. Though not letter quality, the print quality is excellent.

Soft-copy Terminals

Soft-copy or visual display terminals use a display screen. The requested information appears on the screen during a session, then disappears at the end. The display screen is called a cathode ray tube (CRT) or visual display tube (VDT). There are several types:

• Line-by-line mode or "dumb" ASCII (American Standard Code for Information Interchange) terminal. This is the standard workhorse CRT that is used in numerous applications. It can't do anything but display information on its screen and transmit information to its host computer; hence the term "dumb." This device generally operates at speeds ranging from 300 baud to 9600 baud.

• Full-face mode terminal. This terminal differs from the type described above because it has enough memory to store one or more display screens full of data. Its chief distinguishing feature is that it displays the whole screenful of data at once, rather than "line-by-line." As a class, full-face terminals are called *intelligent terminals*, since they often have function keys and some memory.

• Touch panel terminal. A touch panel terminal allows a user to communicate with the computer simply by touching a spot on the screen, rather than typing in instructions on a keyboard. A touch panel can be used with either the line-by-line mode or full-face mode terminals described above. This device appeals to users who think they can't use a computer because they can't type. This factor may be an important aspect of online catalog acceptance, and public and academic libraries that have installed touch terminals in public areas find that users are enthusiastic about them.

Microcomputers as Terminals

Microcomputers are being used in a number of ways for public access to online catalogs. Some online catalogs in small libraries use a microcomputer as the entire system: computer terminal, data storage and patron access. Computer Cat, the online catalog offered by Colorado Computer Systems, Inc., is one example of this.

In the future, many online catalogs may replace the terminals they now use with microcomputers. The microcomputer allows more sophisticated user interfaces with the data base. Unlike other kinds of terminals described above, it may also permit non-Roman character sets to be entered and displayed. RLIN and others are moving in this direction.

Compatibility among Terminals

Just as different pieces of equipment must be compatible, so terminals must be compatible with the online catalog chosen. Some online catalogs, such as the one offered by CLSI, require special terminals, while others use terminal equipment that is more or less standard. The major issues are whether the online catalog system requires:

• Block or full-face mode, or line-by-line mode terminals;

• Special function keys or other features such as cursor control;

• A touch panel.

Some online catalogs are programmed with a particular terminal or family of terminals within a product line in mind. Others can use almost any terminal as long as it follows some standard communications protocol.

THE TELECOMMUNICATIONS LINK

Regardless of where the online catalog computer is located and where the terminals are (unless they are all together in one spot in the library), there must be some pathway by which they are all linked together. This aspect of systems implementation is known as *telecommunications*. There are several options:

• Connect the terminals directly to the computer by cables. This kind of connection is called *hard-wired*. It is usually limited to short distances of a mile or less.

• Use a dial-up connection. This involves linking the terminals with the computer over privately owned or publicly owned telephone lines. The terminal is connected to a *modem* (a device that converts digital signals to analog, and vice versa) which is linked to the telephone. Dial-up connections are relatively easy to install, but they may be expensive if great distances are involved because of the telephone charges that will be incurred. Using a telecommunications network, such as Telenet or Tymnet, terminals from almost any location can be connected to an online catalog located at a network node (communications processor site).

• Use a dedicated line. This connection also involves a telephone line between two points, except that an actual telephone set is not required. A dedicated line is similar to a WATS line in terms of service charges. Costs are generally calculated on a per month basis rather than per connection. A dedicated line may also be used by more than one terminal using a *multiplexer*, a device that allows two or more messages to be transmitted on one line.

All of these types of connections can use standard cable links, microwave links or a combination of the two. The choice of which option to use will depend on the library's own circumstances, and the capabilities and location of the computer system hardware and terminals selected for the online catalog.

BACKUP PLANS

Two of the most frequent questions asked of librarians planning to install an online catalog are: "What happens if the computer is down?" and "What happens to the online catalog if the electricity goes off—how can I use the catalog then?"

It is easier to answer the second question than the first. Most computer systems these days protect themselves against power surges, and most large computer systems have backup power generators. Also, standard data processing procedures prescribe making regular backup copies of the data base; the copies are stored in a remote, secure location so that in the event of a catastrophic power failure (say, lightning hitting the computer room) the data base will be preserved. In the event of a major power outage, the library is likely to be closed anyway, so the fact that the catalog might not be usable for some time will probably not affect many users.

A more serious question is how to handle those times when the computer malfunctions, making the online catalog, for one reason or another, unavailable to patrons and staff. This is called *unplanned downtime*, and it has been a major concern. However, since today's computer equipment is so much more reliable than in the past, unplanned downtime is becoming less of a concern.

Libraries that are still concerned about downtime have several backup options available. First, they can produce a book or microform catalog that can be used in an emergency. This is a deceptively costly choice: although the initial expense may not be great, the cost of frequent updates may be prohibitive. Second, they can install an online catalog with a redundant (backup) hardware configuration. The DataPhase systems that run on Tandem equipment are set up in this way, as are some of the multiprocessor systems from CLSI.

A third option is to ignore the problem. If there is very little unplanned downtime, this is a reasonable solution. Users are quite tolerant of short interruptions in service. The library should be able to protect itself from major systems problems by specifying minimum acceptable performance levels in contractual agreements for the online catalog.

Finally, those libraries that belong to a bibliographic utility, such as OCLC, Research Libraries Group (RLG) or Washington Library Network (WLN), can call up the central data base in these utilities in a pinch if the local online catalog is not working. Although this is a somewhat cumbersome way to get information about the library's holdings, it is another backup that could be used if needed.

ORIENTATION AND TRAINING

Staff Orientation

Although the technical problems of online catalog installation are difficult enough, there is an entirely separate, but related, set of "people problems" that must be overcome if the online catalog is to be a success. The phrase that is most often used to encompass this set of concerns and problems is *management of change*. It deals with all aspects of introducing change—new technology, new procedures, new people and new jobs—in an organization. Ursula Connor reminds us:

> As machines replace human effort, people fear the change as well as their inability to understand the new technology. They fear depersonalization and this feeds their major concern of job security and income. People, just like corporations, have a very real and very necessary concern for their own "bottom line."[3]

Library administrators who are planning online catalogs have a responsibility to their organizations to do as much as they can to overcome the fears and apprehensions of the staff. Here are a few suggestions for easing the way for the online catalog:

• Don't keep the plans a secret. Make sure that the staff is consulted early (and often) about plans for the new online catalog.

• Make it clear that the staff interests and needs are being fully taken into account in the specifications for the new system.

• Give the staff members an opportunity to review and comment on the specifications for the online catalog. Encourage their suggestions and ideas. People are much quicker to accept a new system if they view it as "their" system rather than as something that has been dumped on them.

---

3. Ursula Connor, "Success of Office Automation Depends on User Acceptance, not High Technology," *Computerworld: Special Report* (September 14, 1981): 46-49.

• Explain the concepts of the online catalog. Show how it will affect the staff members' work and show how it will benefit them.

• Plan for enough hands-on experience and training for the staff *before* the system is made available to the public so that the librarians feel comfortable with the online catalog and other new procedures that they may be called upon to use.

Staff and Patron Training

Training for both patrons and staff is as important as proper orientation. Some libraries with online catalogs place the burden of training squarely on the user, while others assume that the library has some responsibility to train users to cope with a new technology. At the Conference on Training Users of Online Catalogs, mentioned earlier, many libraries shared whatever training materials and training programs they developed for patrons and staff.

Even among libraries that take responsibility for patron and staff training, there is a wide difference of opinion on how to proceed. Some libraries have relied upon extensive, formal training programs for everyone, while others believe that an absolute minimum of training is best. In general, the library's own circumstances and user needs will dictate the type of training most appropriate.

Most libraries would agree that the following are the minimum requirements:

• Signs showing where the catalog is;

• Guide cards showing what commands are available;

• Instructions for how to turn the terminal on;

• A brief description of what materials are included in the catalog data base;

• A brief description that gives a conceptual model of how the online catalog works.

The controversy in training centers on more extensive user and staff orientation to online access and how it should be conducted; i.e., training in bibliographic search techniques. Two questions being raised in this area are:

• Does the library have a responsibility to point out to the patron that a "quick and dirty" search may retrieve only a small amount of the library's materials in a given area?

• Is the library responsible for making sure that its staff is thoroughly trained to do or conduct exhaustive searches using the online catalog?

Assuming that the library decides to conduct more extensive training, many questions remain about the best way to proceed. Some of the options are classroom sessions, individual instruction, user manuals and making staff available to answer questions as they arise. Training for online access is a "hot" topic, and many conference sessions, papers, journal articles and discussions will be devoted to it in the near future.

This chapter has concentrated on the different elements that must be considered when installing an online catalog. Chapter 5 reviews the relative costs associated with these elements. The types of online catalogs available and their vendors are described in Chapter 6.

5

Costs and Contracts, Grants and Funding

Cost is a major concern of any library planning to install an online catalog. Although conventional catalogs are far from free, their costs are deeply embedded in budget lines for existing library procedures, personnel and other items. Planning for an online catalog requires measuring these hidden costs (or at least understanding that they exist) so that the cost of an online catalog can be evaluated intelligently.

COSTS OF CONVENTIONAL CATALOGS

The costs involved in maintaining a conventional library catalog differ somewhat according to the form of the catalog; for example, a catalog in book form does not require card cases, and a card catalog does not require microfiche readers. All three options—card catalog, book catalog or computer output (COM) microform catalog—require preparation of catalog records. Card catalogs, of course, have the additional expenses of filing cards, purchasing new card cabinets and providing space for the catalog. Book catalogs have additional expenses associated with both computer costs for producing them and printing costs. Microform catalogs require special processing to create the fiche or film, and readers are needed for patrons and staff.

The start-up and continuing cost components for each of these forms of the conventional catalog are listed in Table 5.1. The start-up costs are relatively small. However, the costs of providing even semi-annual updates to a book or microform catalog can be very high if the catalog is large. Producing supplements simply is not satisfactory; patrons do not use them. In fact, library staff members often do not use them.

The old standby, the card catalog, seems almost to perpetuate itself. It appears to be a small task to slip in a few new cards now and then, but in a library with a large catalog and

Table 5.1: Costs for Forms of the Conventional Catalog

Card Catalog Start-up Costs

    Card cases: $1500 to $2500 each
    Space: varies widely

Card Catalog Continuing Costs

    Cataloging: $0.20 to over $2.00 per item
    Filing: $0.20 to $0.50 per card
    Card cases: $1500 to $2500 each
    Space: varies widely

Book Catalog Start-up Costs

    Retrospective conversion: varies widely
    Computer programming and/or purchased
      services: $0.10 to $0.30 per record; pro-
      gramming at $35.00 to $75.00 per hour

Book Catalog Continuing Costs

    Cataloging: $0.20 to over $2.00 per item
    Computer processing: varies widely depend-
      ing on equipment and fee arrangement
    Printing and binding: $0.05 to $0.10 per page

Microform Catalog Start-up Costs

    Retrospective conversion: varies widely
    Computer programming and/or purchased
      services: $0.10 to $0.30 per record; pro-
      gramming at $35.00 to $75.00 per hour
    Microform readers: $250 and up apiece

Microform Catalog Continuing Costs

    Cataloging: $0.20 to over $2.00 per item
    Computer processing: varies widely
    Microform preparation: $0.15 to $0.50 per
      frame, $0.10 to $0.30 per copy (for
      microfiche)

a large number of new acquisitions, the cost of maintaining the card file is very high indeed. Further, labor costs are high and are rising steadily. Thus, maintaining a card catalog is an expensive option.

COSTS OF AN ONLINE CATALOG

Many components contribute to the cost of an online catalog. The size and type of collection, along with patron and staff needs, will determine the type of online catalog chosen and, in turn, the costs of the final installation. For example, these factors will determine whether a library can choose from among existing systems or will require a custom-made one; the complexity of the online catalog system and the amount of computer capability needed; the number and type of terminals required; and much more. The many variables involved make it impossible to project here what the cost of any particular system will be. However, the major cost areas common to all online catalog systems can be identified, and these are discussed below.

Implementing the System

Whether a library chooses to implement an online catalog by purchasing its own computer, sharing a computer with other libraries or organizations, or purchasing a turnkey system will greatly affect the contributing items (and, therefore, the budget lines) in the total cost package. However, regardless of the method chosen, the overall costs will usually be comparable. This is because whether a library procures the system itself or contracts with a vendor, certain basic items must be paid for.

For example, if the library installs an online catalog system itself, the library pays the computer costs directly. If the library purchases services from a turnkey vendor, the library pays the vendor, who in turn pays the computer manufacturer. When a library contracts for services, the charge is usually one monthly fee that covers everything. The vendor will then pay for the hardware, maintenance, software, software maintenance, telecommunications charges and any other miscellaneous items that arise. If a library chooses to implement the online catalog itself and directly, the library will be responsible for all these costs.

Vendors, of course, must make a profit in order to stay in business, and their fees are structured accordingly. This imposes an additional cost on the library that chooses to purchase turnkey services. Some libraries think they can save money by handling the installation in-house and avoiding the "middle man." However, this too depends on a number of factors, the most important of which is expertise on the part of library staff—both technical expertise and experience in negotiating with individual suppliers. If experienced staff are available, then a library may well save thousands of dollars, especially if what is required is a particularly complex custom-made system.

If a library does not have experienced staff on hand and chooses the in-house route, it risks spending a tremendous amount of time and money only to put together a system that doesn't work properly—as has all too often been the case. In such circumstances, a library is best advised to contract with a turnkey vendor. This, of course, does not rule out negotiation (especially in the area of hardware, where the vendor often starts out charging the list price); nor does it rule out the value of having experienced staff on hand.

Once the method of implementation has been decided, the library must assess the start-up costs involved.

Start-up Costs

The major start-up costs for an online catalog are: computer hardware, software, telecommunications and training. We will discuss computer hardware and software first, since they usually have the largest (and most devastating) effect on the library's budget.

Hardware

Computer hardware prices range from $2000 for a small microcomputer system to well over $2 million for a mainframe. Prices also vary widely depending on the configuration of the particular system. In addition, hardware prices are changing so rapidly that no useful purpose would be served by quoting even approximate prices here. The chief error in forecasting developments in the computer field is the tendency to base predictions on what has been true in the past. Changes in technology and pricing are coming so fast and in such a non-linear fashion that predictions based on what we know today are just not reliable indicators for the future. Nonetheless, a few trends are discernable:

• Cost of computer processing power is decreasing. A dollar spent on computer processing power today will purchase much more next year.

• Cost of online disk storage is decreasing dramatically. For example, online storage that cost $100,000 in 1982 can be purchased for under $20,000 in mid-1983.

• Telecommunications costs are changing. The restructuring of AT&T is affecting this area significantly. Local telecommunications costs are rising, while long distance charges are, in many cases, dropping. Since the area of telecommunications is a volatile one, it will bear close watching.

• The cost of terminals and microcomputers is decreasing steadily. Terminals cost between $300 and $4000 depending on the type of device. Microcomputers suitable for library applications are now available for $2000 to around $15,000. Printers cost from about $800 to more than $5000, depending on print quality and speed. The cost of printers is also declining, but not as rapidly as the cost of terminals and microcomputers.

In addition to the cost of the computer equipment itself, usually there are charges for installation, transportation and insurance. Plan on adding at least 10% to the basic equipment cost to cover these extra expenses. More (much more!) money will be needed if extensive alterations are required to house the equipment. Hardware vendors can tell the library what provisions must be made for the equipment and can estimate the cost. It is important that the physical environment for the equipment meet the vendor's requirements; if it does not, the vendor may refuse to install the equipment or may invalidate any warranties.

Software

The kinds of software needed for the online catalog were described in Chapter 4. As with hardware, there are enormous cost variations, and prices change almost daily. Price ranges for major software components as of early 1983 are listed below.

• Operating system for the computer. As previously noted, this is always required. The cost may range from $200 to $500 for an operating system for a microcomputer to $10,000 to $50,000 for a mainframe operating system. In some cases, the operating system cannot be purchased, but must be leased from the supplier. There often is a relatively high first-year cost followed by a lower continuing cost.

• Data Base Management System (DBMS). In some cases the DBMS may be purchased, in other cases it must be leased. Here again there often is a high first-year cost followed by a lower continuing cost. Purchase or lease costs usually range from $10,000 to $50,000 and up.

• Communications software. Costs for communications software can range from $4000 to $15,000 and up. The software may be purchased or leased.

• Applications programs. Applications software is usually available for purchase from the vendor, although it may only be available for lease or through some kind of licensing agreement. Most of the library turnkey vendor software is available for $20,000 to $60,000 and up; the software cost for some of the microcomputer-based systems is lower, around $3000 to $5000.

• Special programs. The cost of special software varies depending upon the application. The software may be written for a flat fee (say, $5000), or may be billed at the prevailing rate (anywhere from $35 to $75 per hour).

Telecommunications

The library must install enough telecommunications lines to allow patrons and staff access to the online catalog from a number of locations within (and possibly outside) the library. The cost for installing the necessary wiring to support this can be very expensive, ranging from $500 to $1000 for a small system, to the tens of thousands for a large one.

Leased or dedicated lines may have to be installed. The terminals may have to be hard-wired to the computer, or a network such as Telenet or Tymnet may have to be employed. In addition, a library often must purchase modems or other devices. This equipment is expensive and does not seem to be following the downward price trend of other types of computer equipment.

The online catalog vendor can assist the library both in determining what is required and in estimating the costs. However, to be safe, it is wise to double all estimates.

Other Start-up Costs

In addition to the relatively easy-to-measure costs of hardware and software for the online catalog, there is an internal cost to the library that must be taken into account. This will arise as a result of the additional staff time needed to plan, gain approval for and install the online catalog; the cost of conducting training programs; and the cost of developing security backup and disaster recovery plans.

These costs are difficult to measure because they are largely hidden in existing budget lines. Although computers and computer systems are often blamed for eliminating jobs, it is extremely rare that installing a computer system actually reduces the number of people needed to run an organization. The computer system may do away with some tasks (such as filing catalog cards), but usually creates others. Library personnel may find themselves performing somewhat different jobs.

Nevertheless, preparing for this change and ensuring that installation of the online catalog proceeds smoothly, with a minimum of disruption to the organization, is a costly process. Some estimates hold that these hidden costs can equal the cost of the computer hardware and software combined. Because these costs are usually absorbed by longer work days, tighter schedules and busier staff, they rarely show up in the library's budget; yet they do exist and the library must be aware of them in planning for an online catalog.

The cost of training deserves special mention here. It is a major part of the hidden cost to any library involved with installing an online catalog. Training costs are reflected in the need for staff members to work with patrons and other library staff members. Then there are the costs of producing and distributing brochures, guide cards, user manuals and other instructional material. Further, library staff may be asked to conduct workshops, orientation and other programs of bibliographic instruction.

Continuing Costs

Once the online catalog has been installed, the library will have other expenses. These continuing costs may actually be more difficult for the library to pay because they may represent an increase in the library's overall budget. Occasionally, the money a library saves by not having to maintain a conventional catalog will offset the continuing costs of an online catalog, but this is far from guaranteed. The ongoing costs that the library must plan for are discussed below.

Hardware Maintenance

The computer, disk drives, tape drives and other components of the online catalog will all have a monthly maintenance charge. Although these charges may vary from manufacturer to manufacturer and from system to system, a monthly cost of 1% to 2% of the purchase cost of the equipment can be used as a guideline for estimating the annual charges. As an example, maintenance charges for some of the mid-range minicomputers are about $1000 per month. This cost tends to be higher for older equipment and also increases according to the number of hours per day that the system is operating.

Telecommunications

The library will have to pay a continuing cost for the use of communications facilities needed by the online catalog. These may include the cost of phone lines, dedicated lines, modems, data phones and so forth. As noted previously, these costs will most likely continue to rise. Many libraries are investigating the feasibility of using microwave or other nontraditional communications links to cut costs.

Software Maintenance

Frequently, the operating system and other basic software for the online catalog will have a monthly lease charge. This charge covers the cost of periodic updates to the software and any maintenance, and may include a continuing license fee. In addition, the supplier of the applications programs for the online catalog may charge for updates to the system and for future enhancements to the catalog (although this is sometimes included in the maintenance charge). There may also be a continuing cost for any other software needed in the system.

Software maintenance costs can just include initial installation of the program, or can include enhancements or new releases. Thus, the charges can be a relatively small component of the continuing costs or they can equal or exceed the hardware maintenance costs. The philosophy of charging for software has changed over the years. In the early days, computer manufacturers "gave" the software away with the purchase (or lease) of the hardware. Later on, as a result of Federal Trade Commission rulings and various market factors, computer manufacturers began charging separately for the software. Some decided to sell software outright, while others leased the right to use it. In any case, software developers now seek to recover part or all of their costs by imposing continuing charges for software maintenance. Charges range from a few hundred dollars to thousands of dollars a year, depending on the system.

Other Continuing Costs

In a few instances, a vendor that supplies an online catalog as a turnkey system may charge an additional monthly fee to defray its staff expenses for maintaining the system. Other continuing costs include preparation of catalog records for the data base, data base maintenance, and staff and patron orientation and training. The library must also plan to replace the hardware eventually. The useful life of most computer hardware is five to seven years. (Of course, certain pieces of equipment may become obsolete in a shorter time, just as others may last practically a lifetime.) This expenditure should be anticipated and included in the library's budget.

Costs Summary

As the foregoing discussion shows, the actual cost components of an online catalog will vary widely depending on the implementation option chosen. General cost estimates thus serve as only the roughest guidelines. For planning purposes, however, it is useful to have some figure in mind. A *very* small system might cost less than $10,000; a medium-sized system (up to 100,000 items) might cost about $60,000; a minicomputer-based system will cost up to $1 million; and the very large systems such as the ones used by the Online Computer Library Center (OCLC), the Research Libraries Information Network (RLIN) and the Washington Library Network (WLN) cost in the millions of dollars. Table 5.2 can be used as a guide in estimating the likely costs for a particular library and a specific system.

Table 5.2: Checklist of Cost Components for an Online Catalog

Hardware
Central processing unit (CPU), purchase or lease
CPU console
Disk controllers
Disk drives
Equipment maintenance
Equipment replacement
Printers
Tape drives
Terminals
Transportation charges

Software
Applications programs
Communications software
Data base management system
Licenses and fees
Operating system

Program maintenance and future releases
Special purpose programs

Telecommunications
Leased lines
Modems
Telephone equipment and charges

Miscellaneous
Backup plan
Computer operator(s)
Disaster recovery plan
Documentation (user manuals, guides, etc.)
Installation
Insurance
Retrospective conversion
Security
Site preparation
Staff and user training programs
Supplies and consumables

CONTRACTS

Sooner or later, the library will find itself contracting for some type of service in conjunction with its online catalog. The contract might be with a turnkey system vendor, with a computer manufacturer, with a group who will perform retrospective conversion, etc.

Request for Proposal

Prior to any contractual arrangement, and as part of the vendor selection process, the library sends out a Request for Proposal (RFP), which lists all of the library's requirements. This document must be prepared carefully since the vendor will develop the system (or service) according to the RFP's specifications. The following can be used as a guide when preparing an RFP:

• Prior to preparing an RFP, invite several vendors to visit the library and give brief, informational presentations on their offerings. Knowing what vendors have to offer will make preparing the RFP much easier. If there are questions about some of the library's requirements, this is a good time to ask about them: Can any of the vendors support these requirements with existing systems? If not, would they be willing to develop such a system?

• Try to write the RFP as though you had to respond to it. Don't assume that the vendor knows all about your organization. Give the vendor enough information to respond intelligently. Most vendors want to deliver successful systems and try very hard to prepare responsive proposals that will meet the library's needs.

• Decide which criteria will be used to evaluate the proposals, and which of these are most important to the library. Cost? Function? Schedule? Hardware considerations? Vendor performance? Understand that some of the criteria developed for comparing the responses may be important factors in evaluating the proposals, but may not discriminate among the offerings. Therefore, the library may need to develop a second list of factors which, in a sense, are tie-breakers.

Preparing the Contract

Once the library has evaluated the proposals and selected a vendor, the next step is to negotiate the contract. At this point, legal advice will almost certainly be needed. Some libraries may have a staff member with legal training or may be able to use the services of a municipal legal office. An academic or corporate library may have a legal affairs department within the organization.

However, computer law (and, to a large extent, this is what online catalog installations involve) is a relatively new and unknown specialty. The legal affairs office, while understanding contracts law in general terms, may not be able to advise the library on the appropriate safeguards in contracting for online catalog services. In such cases it may be best to use a consultant who has experience with online catalog installations.

Some of the necessary provisions and safeguards in contracts are merely common sense written down, but all too often clients and vendors come to grief over "gentlemen's agreements." Further, what the library means by "acceptable" and what the vendor means by "acceptable" may be vastly different, and some of the worst disputes have arisen because the two parties were using identical words to mean different things.

The following are some guidelines that the library can follow in contractual dealings.

Negotiate

It is vital to read any contract carefully. Don't accept a vendor's contract as is just because it is offered as a "standard" contract. What this means is that the vendor has constructed a document that is intended to protect the vendor in its dealings with libraries—it may not be set up to protect the library. If possible, write the contract yourself so that its bias, if any, will reflect the library's interest instead. Make sure that the stipulations are reasonable and that there are some assurances that the library will get something for its money. This is best accomplished by contacting other libraries that have had online installations and looking at their contracts; by asking or using a consultant; or even by asking a vendor—a good one will tell you whether or not your contract is realistic.

Define Terminology

When drawing up a contract, define all terminology used. This is very important because libraries often use very common terms to mean highly specialized things. It's a good idea to add a section to the contract that defines all the terminology that the library doesn't understand and all the terminology that the vendor doesn't understand. If these terms are made precise, the chances of trouble later on will be reduced.

Be Realistic

Make sure the library's acceptance criteria are realistic. Here again, it's wise to check with other libraries, consultants and vendors. Occasionally, a library will stipulate performance requirements or other provisions that no vendor—no matter how well-intentioned—could possibly meet. In some cases, the vendors simply refuse to bid on the work; in other cases, they go ahead and hope that the contract provisions are never enforced.

Use Caution

Give some thought to the kinds of protections the library requires. The library must have answers to such questions as: What happens if the project is delayed? More than a certain amount of time? What happens if the vendor goes out of business? Before or after the project is completed? For these reasons, the library may have to enlist the aid of a lawyer in reviewing the contract. Make sure the attorney knows enough about the library's needs to represent it effectively.

Don't forget to review the payment schedule carefully. Is it realistic? Is the library actually assured of getting something for the money it is paying out? Would some other schedule be better?

Remember that the best sort of contract is one that is written carefully and intelligently by both parties, signed and sealed, put away and never needed again. The time spent drawing up a good (and workable) agreement with a vendor is time well spent, for it can save the library, its users and its vendors vast amounts of time, trouble and money.

A good overview of contractual agreements is given in *More Joy of Contracts: An Epicurean Approach to Negotiation.*[1] This delightful treatise is written from the standpoint of a library installing an online circulation system, but many of the same provisions are appropriate for an online catalog.

GRANTS AND FUNDING

After estimating costs and choosing vendors, the library is faced with the question of where to get the money. In some public and academic libraries there may be a Friends of the Library group that can provide some of the necessary funds. If the library is extremely fortunate, its parent organization (if any) may allocate the money in the library's budget. Another possibility is for the library to approach a foundation or other public or private source. This last option generally involves preparing a grant application. The remainder of this chapter is intended to help libraries with this process.

Selecting the Appropriate Source

Grant money is usually available to support worthwhile projects. The task facing a library seeking money for an online catalog is to select the appropriate funding sources and to present the project in such a compelling fashion that the agency cannot refuse. This is not as hard as it sounds. Some foundations, such as the Andrew Mellon Foundation and the Sloan Foundation, have millions of dollars to disburse each year, and are continually looking for worthwhile projects to support. If the library can show why its project is special, demonstrate a need and show the likelihood of successful outcome, chances are that some foundation or group of foundations will underwrite the work.

Writing the Proposal

The vehicle by which funding sources are petitioned is the proposal or grant application. A well-written proposal is crucial—in fact, it is often the most important factor in getting the desired funds. A well-written proposal will be clear, free of jargon and relatively brief. It is also important to remember that foundation review committee members may know absolutely nothing about libraries except in the most general terms. Therefore, it is imperative that the ideas presented in the grant application be easily understood without any special knowledge or training.

---

1. Kevin Hegarty, *More Joy of Contracts: An Epicurean Approach to Negotiation* (Tacoma, WA: Tacoma Public Library, 1981).

A good proposal or grant application must be short—most are less than 10 pages long. Clarity is also essential. The library's proposal must present a clear statement of the needs and objectives, and show how the proposed work will address them. Finally, the application should show precisely how the proposed work can be accomplished with the resources on hand and/or being requested, and that it can be accomplished within the schedule set forth.

Remember that the proposal is the main tool that the foundation or other agency will use to evaluate the library's project. If the proposal has been carelessly prepared or if the library has failed to comply with some of its instructions or other provisions, the application may be rejected solely on these grounds without ever being considered on its merits.

Here are a few suggestions for writing successful proposals:

• Read all the forms and instructions carefully. Make a checklist to ensure that all the requirements are being met. Have a library staff member who is not involved with the project review the application to make sure that it meets the requirements and describes the project accurately.

• Write with clarity and precision. Remember that the reviewers are busy people; they need to understand quickly what the proposal is about and what you are asking for.

• Use only language that will be understandable to the funding agency. Clarify anything that is not obvious to the reader and avoid jargon and technical terms. If you must use technical terms, define them. It helps to have someone who is unfamiliar with libraries and not associated with the project review the proposal to ensure that it is understandable to non-librarians and non-technical readers.

• Explain all abbreviations and acronyms.

• Do everything possible to make the proposal readable. Make the significant points at the outset and make it easy for the reader to find the heart of the request. Use underlining and other formatting devices to draw attention to important points.

The proposal or grant application may contain a number of different sections. Some of these may be required by the funding agency while others will be suggested by the nature of the request. A proposal for an online catalog might include the following:

• Title page—select a title that describes the work to be done.

• Abstract or executive summary—a very brief statement describing the request. It should include how much money is being requested.

• Introduction—sets the environment for the request. It can be quite brief or can include some background information, if necessary.

- Objective or statement of need—sets forth the purpose of the project and describes the need.

- Approach or procedure—describes how the work will be carried out. This may consist of two sections: a general description and a list of tasks to be carried out.

- Budget—should enumerate the anticipated costs, but not in too much detail. The detailed costs can be included in an appendix.

- Schedule—the timetable according to which the work described will be performed.

Any other detailed information or supporting documentation can usually be included in appendixes. This keeps the main document short, while providing the supporting documentation if any reviewers wish to see it.

If the library has access to someone who is experienced in grant preparation, the proposal should be reviewed by that person before submission. Further, an experienced grant writer may be able to suggest appropriate funding sources to contact, and may know the range of grants that each can support. For example, it would be fruitless to ask for $100,000 from a foundation if it has only $20,000 to give away each year.

Remember also that funding from a grant can often be used to get matching funds. If you are successful in getting one grant, you may be able to use it to get matching funds from other sources. Be creative, explore all options and above all, do not get discouraged. The old adage "if at first you don't succeed..." is especially true in getting grant support. The reasons grant applications are turned down by foundations are many and various and may have nothing to do with the worth of the project. Keep trying—sooner or later the application will be successful.

6

Choosing an Online Catalog

As of mid-1983 there were approximately 30 known online catalog systems of one sort or another in the United States and Canada. Some of these are merely online circulation systems with some online inquiry features; and a few others, while providing some online catalog features, were not designed for public access. For the sake of completeness, however, they are all listed in Table 6.1. (See also Appendixes D and E.) If any system has been omitted, it is because a search of the literature and conversations with colleagues and vendors failed to turn up mention of it. However, readers should remember that this field is changing extremely rapidly, and new systems will undoubtedly be available by the time this book is published.

It is important to note that only some of the systems listed in Table 6.1 are actually operating as online catalogs now, and not all of them are available for installation in other locations. However, all are at least fairly far along in the development process, and many have been installed for several years. In most instances, the online catalog is one component of a larger system—often an integrated library system or library information system.

The following section describes the online catalog component of representative systems. All the systems described here are operational and available for transfer from commercial vendors or from the library where installed and/or developed. Specifications and prices are as of mid-1983, and changes should be expected. After describing particular systems, we will offer some guidelines for libraries attempting to choose among the options available.

Libraries seeking additional information may wish to consult the survey by Joseph R. Matthews, *Public Access to Online Catalogs*, which describes systems that are not available for transfer as well as those that are.[1] Charles R. Hildreth's *Online Public Access*

---

1. Joseph R. Matthews, *Public Access to Online Catalogs: A Planning Guide for Managers* (Weston, CT: Online, Inc., 1982).

Table 6.1: Online Catalog Systems

Vendor or Institution	System Name
Advanced Data Management	BiblioTech
Beth-Israel Hospital	PaperChase
Biblio-Techniques	Biblio-Techniques Library & Information System (BLIS)
Carlyle Systems, Inc.	The Online Multiple User System (TOMUS)
CL Systems, Inc. (CLSI)	Public Access Catalog (PAC)
Claremont Colleges	Total Library System (TLS)
Colorado Computer Systems, Inc. (Computer Cat)	Computer Cat
CTI Library Systems, Inc.	Esprit Systems
Dallas Public Library	LSCAN
Dartmouth College	Online Catalog
DataPhase Systems, Inc.	ALIS II—Public Access Catalog (PAC)
Data Research Associates	A Total Library Automated System (ATLAS)
DTI Data Trek, Inc.	Card Datalog
Easy Data Systems Ltd.	Integrated Library System
Geac Canada Ltd.	Library Information System
IBM	DOBIS/LEUVEN
Jefferson County Public Library	Jeffcat
Library of Congress	SCORPIO/MUMS
Minnesota State University System	Data Access System
National Library of Medicine, National Technical Information Service Online Computer Systems, Inc. Avatar Systems, Inc.	Integrated Library System (ILS)
Northwestern University	NOTIS/LUIS
Online Computer Library Center, Inc. (OCLC)	OCLC
Ohio State University	Library Control System (LCS)
Pikes Peak Library District	Maggie's Place
Research Libraries Group (RLG)	Research Libraries Information Network (RLIN)
Southeastern Library Information Network (SOLINET)	Local Access to and Management of Bibliographic Data and Authorities (LAMBDA)
Syracuse University Libraries	Syracuse University Libraries Information System (SULIRS)
Universal Library Systems	Universal Library Systems (ULISYS)
University of California	MELVYL
University of New Brunswick	Phoenix
University of Toronto Library Automated Systems (UTLAS)	Library Collection Management System (LCMS)
Virginia Tech Library Automation Project	Virginia Tech Library System (VTLS)
Washington State Library	Washington Library Network (WLN)
Washington University School of Medicine	Bibliographic Access and Control System (BACS)

Catalogs is required reading for anyone undertaking an exhaustive comparison of the features of online catalogs.[2] Libraries are also strongly urged to contact individual vendors directly. Most vendors are delighted to arrange an on-site demonstration, and this is by far the best way to get an idea of how each system works. Vendors also exhibit and demonstrate their systems at national meetings, such as those sponsored by the American Library Association (ALA), the Special Libraries Association (SLA) or the American Society for Information Science (ASIS). New features and products are often first announced at these meetings.

ADVANCED DATA MANAGEMENT
c/o Comstow Information Services
302 Boxboro Rd.
Stow, MA 01775
(617) 897-7163
Contact: Lynda W. Moulton

Advanced Data Management offers a family of computer software packages for special libraries and information centers. It uses DRS, a data base management system, as the foundation for the BiblioTech software. The system runs on Digital Equipment Corp. (DEC) computers, such as the PDP 11/24 through PDP 11/70, and the VAX line of minicomputers. Although library patrons can use the BiblioTech system, it was really designed with the needs of the technical librarian/information specialist in mind.

The BiblioTech software permits searching in a variety of fields including author, title, subject heading and call number (to mention a few); according to Ms. Moulton, these may be combined using Boolean operators. Keyword searching and right-hand truncation are supported, but there are no proximity indicators.

The BiblioTech programs enable libraries to create their own catalog records, modify or delete records, and produce a variety of hard-copy reports. The system supports authority file maintenance, acquisitions and circulation control. Other functional modules, such as serials check-in, claiming, routing and binding, are under development.

The cost of implementing a BiblioTech system depends heavily on the choice of hardware, the size of the files involved and the record format selected. The BiblioTech software is priced independently of the hardware and also may be acquired module by module. The online catalog module is $20,000 for a multiple-user system.

BIBLIO-TECHNIQUES
8511 Lake Lucinda Dr. SW
Olympia, WA 98502
(206) 786-1111
Contact: Richard Woods

Biblio-Techniques is a turnkey vendor marketing the software developed by the Washington Library Network (WLN). The system runs on IBM or IBM-compatible

2. Charles R. Hildreth, *Online Public Access Catalogs: The User Interface* (Dublin, OH: OCLC Library, Information, and Computer Science Series, 1982).

equipment and uses ADABAS as the underlying data base manager. The Biblio-Techniques Library and Information System (BLIS) is an integrated library system that provides online cataloging, authority control, catalog management and acquisitions/accounting support. Biblio-Techniques has developed an Easy Access mode to provide online catalog searching for patrons and infrequent catalog users.

Because the system runs on mainframe equipment, it has been installed as a shared system used by several libraries within a region. The Southeastern Library Information Network (SOLINET), for example, is using the WLN software for its Local Access to and Management of Bibliographic Data and Authorities (LAMBDA) system. This system is designed to meet the needs of 11 libraries in the Atlanta, GA, area.

Cost of the BLIS software package ranges from $300,000 to $350,000 depending on the operating system selected. Biblio-Techniques can provide hardware and software or software-only systems with full installation, training and maintenance support services.

CARLYLE SYSTEMS, INC.
600 Bancroft Way
Berkeley, CA 94710
(415) 843-3538
Contact: Steve Salmon

Carlyle Systems offers an online patron access catalog system called The Online Multiple User System (TOMUS). TOMUS runs on IBM or IBM-compatible mainframes. In its present form, it is most suitable for very large libraries or for groups of libraries in a university-wide or regional setting. The TOMUS software can be licensed for $100,000. Carlyle is developing a new version of TOMUS, which it says will be less expensive and can be installed as a stand-alone system or shared by several libraries. The new version is scheduled to be available in late fall 1983.

CL SYSTEMS, INC.
81 Norwood Ave.
Newtonville, MA 02160
(617) 965-6310
Contact: Susan Stearns

CL Systems, Inc. (CLSI) is one of the pioneers in online library systems. CLSI's Public Access Catalog (PAC) is part of its LIBS 100 online circulation system. The system runs on DEC minicomputers. Often the PDP 11/34 is used, but other CPUs in the same series may be appropriate for smaller or larger libraries.

CLSI's LIBS 100 system uses the now-famous "touch panel" so that users do not have to key in data. Recent enhancements to the CLSI software, however, let users key in certain search parameters to allow search terms to be combined during the initial request and to assist with the use of Boolean operators. The CLSI system uses a terminal with touch pad, standard keyboard and function key capabilities. Users may choose the mode of use that best suits their purposes.

The CLSI Public Access Catalog was first installed in the Evanston (IL) Public Library in October 1980. It was the first library in the country to use the touch panel approach to online access.

Since that time, CLSI has added many new search features to its online catalog subsystem. These enhancements are usually made available to CLSI customers in releases; the latest (1982-1983) is release 26. CLSI adds new features to its system in response to user suggestions and problems. In addition, CLSI offers libraries the choice of adopting certain enhancements or remaining with the release currently being used. This is because an enhancement needed by one library might not be needed by another and might, in fact, be undesirable.

The CLSI software costs about $50,000 depending on the components needed. Because new releases come out quite frequently, this review will not attempt to list the capabilities of CLSI's online catalog system. A call to the local CLSI representative is the best way to find out what features are currently being offered.

CLAREMONT COLLEGES LIBRARY
800 Dartmouth Ave.
Claremont, CA 91711
(714) 621-8045
Contact: Pat Barkey

The Claremont Colleges Library Total Library System (TLS) was developed locally and is now being marketed by the Online Computer Library Center, Inc. (OCLC). The system runs on a Hewlett-Packard minicomputer. The cost of the system varies with the size of the data base and the number of terminals needed.

The search activity employs implicit right-hand truncation—the user is asked to type in at least three letters or as much as is known of the author, title or other search key. Combined searches involving author, title and subject fields are permitted. The TLS software package costs from $35,000 to $45,000.

COLORADO COMPUTER SYSTEMS, INC.
3005 W. 74th Ave.
Westminster, CO 80030
(303) 426-5880
Contact: Warren Magdanz

Colorado Computer Systems, Inc. markets Computer Cat, a microcomputer-based online catalog designed and developed for an elementary school library. The system runs on an Apple II+ microcomputer. It has reportedly been used successfully in the Mountain View Elementary School in Broomfield, CO, for whom it was developed. It was installed in December 1980, and is now being marketed to other libraries. The cost of the software is $995 for a single user system, and $1195 for a multi-user system.

CTI LIBRARY SYSTEMS, INC.
120 E. 300 North
Provo, UT 84061
(801) 373-0344
Contact: Jim Wilson

CTI Library Systems, Inc. offers a turnkey automated integrated library system. The system is an outgrowth of an online circulation system that was developed for Brigham Young University. The total system includes an online circulation subsystem and an online catalog. An acquisitions system is being tested and an online serials receipt control system is planned for introduction early in 1984.

The CTI system runs on Microdata minicomputers or on a variety of Prime minicomputers. The Prime-based systems use the INFORMATION data base manager marketed by Prime and the PRIMOS operating system. CTI will provide an entire turnkey package including hardware, software, installation and training, or whatever portions the library needs.

The circulation and online catalog systems are menu-driven, and it is easy for a new user to learn to operate either system. Further, the system is well-protected, with a series of password and other control features, from unauthorized (or unexpected) modification of the data base.

The cost of the CTI system varies depending on the hardware requirements. The software costs range from $15,000 to $50,000 depending on the subsystems and operating system selected, and whether the components are purchased together or separately.

CTI Library Systems, Inc. is affiliated with the Government Systems Group, Inc., Albany, NY.

DATAPHASE SYSTEMS, INC.
3770 Broadway
Kansas City, MO 64111
(816) 931-7927
Contact: Bruce Gelb or Sara Hill

DataPhase offers a turnkey automated library system called ALIS II. The system can run on the Data General Eclipse minicomputers or the Tandem minicomputer depending on the size of the library and the anticipated volume of circulation. The system on Data General uses the MUMPS operating system; on Tandem, it uses COBOL.

ALIS II has the ability to load, store and access full MARC records. Users can search for author, title, subject, call number, ISBN, ISSN and other fields. In addition, a key word search may be made over subject headings, and combined author/title and author/subject Boolean searches are possible. The system provides for an authority control file and an authority maintenance capability.

The ALIS II system is an integrated library system that has grown out of an online circulation system. It now includes online public access, online cataloging, online circulation, authority control and booking. An acquisitions subsystem is being developed. A version of the system demonstrated in January 1983 features a touch panel that lets users indicate their choices without keying data. A keyboard is available, however, so the patron can enter any needed data directly.

The cost of the system depends on the configuration required. On Data General equipment, the ALIS II software costs $40,000 and the operating system costs $15,000. For the Tandem system, the cost is approximately $100,000.

DARTMOUTH COLLEGE LIBRARY
Dartmouth College
Hanover, NH 03755
(206) 646-2574
Contact: Emily G. Fayen

The Dartmouth College Library online public access catalog system was the result of a cooperative effort between Bibliographic Retrieval Services (BRS) and Dartmouth College. The system uses BRS/Search as the underlying software. Dartmouth developed a user-friendly interface to make the catalog suitable for public access.

The system provides full keyword searching over the entire bibliographic record. The Boolean operators AND, OR and NOT are fully supported, as well as the positional operators WITH, SAME, ADJ and NEAR. Range searching (searching on a range of numbers such as publication dates, author's birthdate, OCLC number) is permitted on numeric fields.

At Dartmouth, the system is running on a DEC VAX 11/750 minicomputer under the UNIX operating system. It will run on any equipment that supports UNIX or UNIX-emulators, such as UNIQ. The online catalog will run on microcomputers or on a wide range of minicomputers. The Dartmouth online catalog contains more than 400,000 records and can be accessed from more than 300 terminals on campus, or from other locations using a dial-up connection.

BRS is marketing the combined package, which includes the BRS software and the Dartmouth interface. The price ranges from well under $10,000 for a microcomputer-based system, to about $50,000 for a minicomputer system supporting more than 8 terminals.

DATA RESEARCH ASSOCIATES
9270 Olive Blvd.
St. Louis, MO 63132
(800) 325-0888 or in Missouri (314) 432-1100
Contact: James Michael

Data Research Associates (DRA) has developed a system for libraries called A Total Library Automated System (ATLAS). Among the functions it supports are circulation, acquisitions, public online catalog, cataloging, serials receipt control (in progress), material booking (in progress), and information and referral. DRA also has software that will produce newspaper indexes, a union list of serials, COM catalogs and printed library catalogs.

The first installation of ATLAS was in the Cleveland Public Library. A second major installation, for the Buffalo & Erie County Public Library, is nearing completion.

The system runs on DEC VAX minicomputers. It uses the MARC data base manager developed by DRA. The DRA software runs on a standard CRT terminal with touch pad and full keyboard. It can be used from any terminal connected to the system and does not require any special-purpose hardware.

DRA's public access catalog allows users to conduct searches for author, title and subject entries in the library catalog. There are two searching modes: a browsing mode, designed for the less experienced patron, and a direct lookup mode. In the browsing mode, patrons use a touch keypad to search the online catalog data base in a manner analogous to searching the alphabetized card catalog drawers. Selection is then made from a display of alphabetized entries. This search can be repeated to narrow the list of possible matches. A list of hits is displayed from which the user can select specific titles for complete or partial display along with status information for each copy of the title.

In direct lookup mode, the patron may type in all or part of an author's name, title or subject heading. Once the set of hits has been identified, the patron can view the titles as described in the browsing mode.

There is no provision for Boolean operators and no support for keyword lookup in the current version of the PAC software. DRA is working on enhancements to PAC that will add the capability to use Boolean operators, have additional search fields and provide authority control.

The cost for the total ATLAS software package is $60,000. Individual modules can be ordered separately.

DTI DATA TREK, INC.
121 West E St.
Encinitas, CA 92024
(619) 436-5055
Contact: Scot Cheatham

DTI Data Trek has developed Card Datalog, a turnkey, microcomputer-based automated library system aimed at meeting the needs of corporate libraries. It includes modules that support an online catalog, acquisitions system, serials control and a laboratory notebook subsystem. The systems installed in special libraries have online patron access capability.

Card Datalog runs on any microcomputer using a CP/M or MS/DOS operating system. Cost of installing the DTI system varies depending on the size of the application and hence the size of the microcomputer and disk drive needed. The price of the online catalog module is about $2400.

EASY DATA SYSTEMS LTD.
401-1200 Lonsdale Ave.
North Vancouver, British Columbia V7M 3H6
(604) 986-8261
Contact: Oliver Pesch

Easy Data Systems Ltd. is a turnkey library system vendor that has offered a system supporting circulation, cataloging and acquisitions. Recent enhancements to its search software permit better online inquiry. Thus, the firm is now offering its system for online patron access.

The Easy Data system runs on Datapoint minicomputers. The software is available for approximately $60,000.

GEAC CANADA LTD.
350 Steelcase Rd. West
Markham, Ontario Canada L3R 1B3
(416) 495-0525 or in the U.S. (203) 877-1486
Contact: Lewis Lenese

Geac markets an online Library Information System developed in conjunction with the University of Guelph (Guelph, Ontario). The system started as an online circulation system and soon grew to include an acquisitions system and an online catalog, as well as the ability to add catalog data locally or from a utility. The Geac system runs on Geac computers, which were developed especially for large online data base applications such as the online catalog.

The Geac system can accommodate full MARC records and can support name and subject authority files. Online catalog users can search by the usual author, title and subject entry points and can also do keyword searches and searches using Boolean operators.

The cost of the Geac software is about $35,000 for the total system.

IBM CORP.
10401 Fernwood Rd.
Bethesda, MD 20034
(301) 897-2059
Contact: Frank Benham

IBM, working with the Dortmund Library System in Germany and the Leuven Library System in Belgium, has developed an automated library system called DOBIS/LEUVEN. The combined DOBIS/LEUVEN system supports circulation, acquisitions, cataloging and online catalog search for both librarians and patrons, using keywords (titles, conferences and corporations, authors, and subjects).

The system runs on IBM mainframe equipment (such as the IBM 370/138) under either the OS/VS or DOS/VSE operating system. The software can be leased for about $36,000 for the DOS/VSE version and about $50,000 for the OS/VS version, for a period of 24 months. At the end of that time, the library has a paid-up license for the software.

MANKATO STATE UNIVERSITY
Minnesota State University System
Mankato, MN 56001
(507) 389-6201
Contact: Dale K. Carrison

The online catalog developed at Mankato State University in Minnesota is now serving nine libraries. The online catalog data base contains records for over 740,000 titles representing a collection of about 1.4 million volumes. More than 140 terminals are linked directly with the library's computer, and other users have dial-up access from numerous remote locations. The system runs on Univac Computers.

Mankato is reportedly working on authority file enhancements (to be available in late 1983) and additional modules for a planned integrated system. The next portions of the system to be implemented will be acquisitions and serials control, followed by online circulation. Each of these modules will be available separately to libraries that have installed the online catalog.

The online catalog system software is available from Mankato State University and costs approximately $20,000.

NATIONAL LIBRARY OF MEDICINE
National Technical Information Service (NTIS)
5275 Port Royal Rd.
Springfield, VA 22161
(703) 487-4807
Contact: Charles Goldstein   (301) 496-1936

The National Library of Medicine sponsored development of an Integrated Library System (ILS) for its own use. This system is available directly from National Technical Information Service (NTIS) and also from at least two commercial vendors, Avatar Systems, Inc. (Potomac, MD) and Online Computer Systems, Inc. (Germantown, MD).

The Integrated Library System uses the MUMPS operating system. The system runs on a variety of DEC, Data General and IBM minicomputers. Avatar and Online Systems, Inc. have each made many modifications to the basic system. These changes have generally added new features and made the system easier to use (more "user friendly").

ILS was intended from the outset to be an integrated system, and the approach to data base design and content arose from that premise. Full MARC records are supported, and, in at least one version of the system, online cataloging, circulation, public access, authority control and acquisitions are supported. Plans are underway to add serials receipt control.

Because the ILS was developed by a library for its own use, it has many features (such as the authority control support) that are especially attractive to librarians. It is especially well-suited for applications involving multiple libraries, where much of the system use will handle library-to-library transactions.

The ILS software is available from NTIS approximately at cost, or about $2700. The enhanced packages from the vendors sell for about $50,000.

NORTHWESTERN UNIVERSITY
1935 Sheridan Rd.
Evanston, IL 60201
(312) 492-7640
Contact: John McGowan

Northwestern University has been deeply involved with library automation since the early 1970s and was one of the first libraries in the country to have an operational integrated online library system and an online catalog. The total system is called Northwestern On-Line Total Integrated System (NOTIS) and the online catalog component is called Library User Information Service (LUIS).

The system runs on an IBM 4331 computer and the programs are primarily written in assembly language and COBOL. The system supports full MARC records with full authority control. In addition to the online catalog subsystem, there are components that support cataloging, acquisitions, serials receipt control and circulation.

The online catalog permits users to search by author, author/title, title/author, subject and ISSN. Northwestern library users can determine bibliographic and holdings information, including current periodical issue availability, and can then request status information from the circulation system. The search procedures assume automatic right-hand truncation, so the user need enter only a few beginning characters of an author name or title word to begin the search. If the search retrieves more than 17 entries, a summary of the index, or guide, is presented. Brief format displays of the citations are available once a set of desired items has been identified. Subject access proceeds in the same manner with the additional feature that users can specify the type of subject heading to be searched.

The NOTIS system includes more than 500,000 records for monographs cataloged since 1971 and all serials. It supports more than 70 terminals. A growing file of authority records will be available to users for cross-reference information.

Northwestern makes the software available to other institutions for $50,000.

PIKES PEAK REGIONAL LIBRARY DISTRICT
PO Box 1579
Colorado Springs, CO 80901
(303) 473-2080
Contact: Kenneth E. Dowlin

This regional library set out in 1975 to develop an automated library system for its own use. Called Maggie's Place, the system supports a host of library management functions and online public access. In addition, users can use the system to get information on community events, adult education, carpools and clubs. There are also some game programs that library patrons may use.

Although Maggie's Place was not specifically designed as an online catalog, it has been successfully used as such for several years now. The system runs on DEC PDP 11/70 minicomputers. The software costs about $20,000.

UNIVERSAL LIBRARY SYSTEMS
1571 Bellevue Ave.
West Vancouver, British Columbia
Canada V7V 1A5
(604) 926-7421
Contact: Jim Speight

Universal Library Systems markets an integrated library system called ULISYS. This system is an outgrowth of an online circulation system developed for Mission College and West Valley Community College (CA). The software runs on DEC PDP 11 series computers under the RSTS/E operating system. The programs are written in BASIC+.

The public access catalog portion of the system has been in use since April 1980. Users may search by author, title, author/title, subject headings, call number, and by course and instructor for items located in the reserve collection. As a turnkey system, the cost varies depending on the hardware requirements and functions selected for implementation. The system is available on a software-only basis for a total cost of $95,000. This price includes the software itself ($65,000); implementation services, such as building the data base, training, etc. ($20,000); and any modifications needed to customize the software ($10,000).

VIRGINIA TECH LIBRARY AUTOMATION PROJECT
113 Burruss Hall
Blacksburg, VA 24061
(703) 961-5847
Contact: Carl Lee

The Virginia Tech Library System (VTLS) was developed in 1976 to provide online circulation control and online search facilities for the Virginia Tech Library. The system uses a Hewlett-Packard minicomputer running under MPE IV and the programs are in COBOL.

The system can accept records in brief or full MARC format. It provides authority control, and users can search the data base by author, title, author/title, subject heading, series and other fields.

The online catalog is part of a total system that includes circulation, acquisitions and serials receipt. Software for the system costs $20,000.

BIBLIOGRAPHIC UTILITIES

In addition to the online catalog systems described above, there are the bibliographic utilities such as the Online Computer Library Center, Inc. (OCLC), the Research Libraries Information Network (RLIN), the Washington Library Network (WLN), the University of Toronto Automated Library Systems (UTLAS), the Southeastern Library Information Network (SOLINET) and others. These utilities exist primarily to provide cataloging data to their member organizations. Virtually all of them now offer some type of online patron access to their data bases, and some, such as WLN, have made their software available to other libraries. In 1983 OCLC entered into an arrangement with Online Computer Systems, Inc. to provide an automated library system based on the National Library of Medicine's ILS system. The new system, called the LS/2000, will be marketed by OCLC and will support an online public access catalog, in addition to other functions.

OCLC plans to install the system in fall 1983 for Five Colleges, Inc. (Amherst College, Hampshire College, Mount Holyoke College, Smith College and University of Massachusetts) and for the Dublin Cluster (University of Akron, Ohio Wesleyan University, Hampshire College and the OCLC Corporate Library). The system will be commercially available in January 1984. In addition, OCLC announced in summer 1983 its intent to acquire Avatar, Inc., the other vendor that has marketed and made enhancements to the ILS system upon which the LS/2000 is based.

CHOOSING THE BEST SYSTEM

With so many online catalog systems now available, it may be difficult to select the one best suited to meet a library's needs. A number of factors have been used to compare the various systems. Some of these factors are not particularly useful in evaluating the systems, and some no longer serve as very effective criteria in distinguishing among the offerings. However, they are the only means we have of indicating the differences among the various online catalogs and showing how these differences affect performance. The factors we shall examine are dialog mode, search features, access points, display features and hardware requirements.

DIALOG MODE

Menu or Command

The earliest online catalog systems were based on a pure menu- or pure command-driven approach. In a menu-driven system, the user options are always presented as a choice among pre-specified items. Figure 6.1 shows a typical menu display.

In a command-driven system, the user enters instructions to the system using a pre-specified syntax, but the options are not necessarily defined ahead of time. Figure 6.2 shows a typical set of commands to an online catalog.

Early online catalog dialog modes were limited to either menu- or command-driven approaches primarily because systems designers believed that one mode was superior to the other. As we have learned more about how users want to interact with an online catalog, it has become apparent that a hybrid approach may be preferable. This is because new or

Figure 6.1: A Menu Display from the CLSI System

```
HELLO

WELCOME TO EVANSTON PUBLIC LIBRARY'S NEW PUBLIC ACCESS CATALOG (PAC)

THIS IS A TOUCH SENSITIVE TERMINAL WHICH PROVIDES UP-TO-DATE
LISTINGS OF THE LIBRARY'S HOLDINGS BY AUTHOR AND TITLE.
SUBJECT ACCESS WILL BE GRADUALLY ADDED DURING THE YEAR.

WE HOPE THAT YOU WILL ENJOY USING IT.
LIBRARIANS WILL BE HAPPY TO ASSIST YOU.

AUTHOR
TITLE
SUBJECT

START                                                         HELP
OVER
                                                         CL SYSTEMS
```

infrequent users of the online catalog have different needs from experienced or frequent users of the catalog. New users need the assistance of the step-by-step menu approach, while more experienced users may be bored or frustrated by the tedium of continually going through menus. A hybrid approach, giving the user the choice of a menu- or command-driven interface, may be the best option. Many of the newer online catalogs, such as those offered by DataPhase, CLSI and DRA, do use such a combined approach to their user interfaces.

Touch Panel, Function Keys or Keyboard

Another controversy arises over the type of terminal that is best for online catalog users. The two extremes are the touch panel and the keyboard. As discussed in Chapter 2, the touch panel requires no keying of data and therefore is especially welcomed by children, the elderly and others for whom typing does not come easily. However, it can be frustrat-

Figure 6.2: A Set of Commands to the MELVYL System

```
FIND PA JAMES, HENRY AND TI WINGS

FIND TI MAGIC OR SU MAGIC

BROWSE SU ALCOHOL AND NOT FUEL

DISPLAY 1 2 3 LONG
```

ing to experienced users who find themselves stepping screen-by-screen through the program when they know that one quick statement entered on a keyboard could identify the information they want.

The use of function keys represents a sort of middle ground. The intent here is to cut down the amount of typing and to make it easy for a new user to communicate with the system simply by selecting an appropriate key. Function keys may be used with either menu-driven or command-driven systems.

As with menu- and command-driven systems, the trend seems to be toward a hybrid approach. CLSI has added some keyboard capabilities to its touch panel system. Other vendors, such as DataPhase, have added a touch panel to their terminals. The important thing to bear in mind in evaluating online catalog systems is whether such special features as touch panels and function keys really make the system easier to use or merely add to the cost of the terminals. There is no question that these features are expensive; on the other hand, they may more than make up for the increased cost by providing significantly better service.

Brief or Full Prompts

Some online catalog systems allow the user to select either a brief or a full set of the dialog and system messages. Obviously, this option is an attempt to meet the needs of both new and more experienced users. This feature seems to work quite well—especially if the user can switch from one form to the other at any time.

SEARCH FEATURES

Search features are perhaps the best discriminators to use for identifying the differences among various online catalogs. Although some of the features may have different names, their effects on retrieval may be identical. In this section, search options that cause the same outcome are grouped together, regardless of the name used to describe them. The features included here were defined in Chapter 1. This section will examine the desirable and undesirable aspects of each.

Keyword or Free-text Searching

As explained in Chapter 1, keyword or free-text searching means that each individual word of a bibliographic citation may be retrieved *by itself*. Some online catalogs, such as the Dartmouth system, make the entire bibliographic citation searchable in this manner while others limit the use of this feature to certain fields, such as title or subject. When keyword searching is combined with Boolean operators, it provides the most flexible and powerful retrieval of all.

Phrase Searching

Many of the online catalog systems that have separate indexes for personal names, corporate names, subject headings, series titles, etc. are using phrase searching. This means that the fields in the record are indexed in the data base as phrases rather than as individual words.

Phrase searching requires the user to supply an entire name, subject, title or other element that will be matched against the appropriate index or indexes in the online catalog data base. Thus, the request usually must be worded as it is represented in the appropriate index. For example, a patron looking for Ernest Hemingway's *The Old Man and the Sea* would ask the system to look for HEMINGWAY, ERNEST and OLD MAN AND THE SEA. The process is analogous to what would be required in the card catalog and does not present a problem for many searches. In addition, as pointed out in Chapter 1, phrase searching is useful for providing a restrictive retrieval capability.

But consider the case of a patron searching for a more complex author name, for example, "Sir James Phillips Kay-Shuttleworth, 1804-1877." Is the entry under SHUTTLE-WORTH, KAY or KAY-SHUTTLEWORTH? In an online catalog with phrase searching only, a patron searching for names might have to look in several places to find the desired entry.

Or consider the following example: entries for "Friedrich Heinrich Emmanuel Kayser" appear under KAYSER, EMMANUEL instead of KAYSER, FRIEDRICH, as one would expect. Fortunately, there is a cross-reference to this effect in the card catalog, and it is precisely because of irregularities such as this (and the restrictive qualities of phrase searching) that many librarians insist on authority file cross-reference information in their online catalogs. Note, however, that a *keyword* search on FRIEDRICH KAYSER would find the desired entries, regardless of the authorized form of the name.

Truncation

Many online catalogs that use phrase searching also use truncation; i.e., the user need enter only the first few letters of the desired phrase and the system will use those to locate and display the appropriate part of the indexes. Some systems display a list of index entries beginning with the characters specified, while others display a list of entries surrounding the characters specified. This latter form is very helpful—especially if the patron has made a minor misspelling in the entry that prevents an exact match from being made.

Truncation may also be used in a very powerful way in online catalogs that have keyword or free-text searching. In this case, the truncation feature can be used to indicate that variant suffixes or roots are wanted. This eliminates a great deal of typing and can enhance retrieval results significantly.

Boolean Operators

Boolean operators, as discussed in Chapter 1, are the combining factors that make post-coordinated retrieval possible. Online catalog systems that use phrase searching often do not have the capability of performing true Boolean combinations of retrieved document sets. They may have combined indexes for author/title and other elements, but they usually cannot support Boolean operators over more than a few fields.

As previously indicated, the advantage of Boolean operators is the power and flexibility they give the user in identifying materials of interest. The disadvantage heretofore was that most systems with this capability could only be implemented on very large mainframe computers, and thus were extremely expensive to develop and to operate. Now, however, several minicomputer-based systems—such as those offered by Avatar, CTI, CLSI and DataPhase—have this capability.

Derived Search Keys

Some online catalog systems use derived search keys to identify sets of citations that meet certain retrieval criteria. The derived search key is one way of creating combined author/title and other indexes without using the amounts of storage needed to support full Boolean logic. The Claremont Colleges online catalog, for example, uses these search keys for retrieval.

The advantages of this approach are that it is an efficient data base organization technique (i.e., doesn't use up much memory), and it provides extremely rapid retrieval over very large data bases. The primary disadvantage is that it is not very natural for the user—generally, users must be instructed in the procedures for constructing the search key. Further, on occasion the search key constructed by the user retrieves a set of citations that is so large that the system cannot display all the records. Also, while some systems can make the request more precise (for example, by combined keyword searching), others cannot.

Other Search Features

Many of the online catalog systems have additional search features. Some features provide a means of storing search results as the session proceeds; others provide ways to limit the results of a search by various factors such as language, publication date and so forth. Most of these have been examined in great detail in Hildreth's work, mentioned earlier, and thus will not be repeated here. Still, for a serious examination of the alternatives, there is no substitute for actual hands-on experience through a vendor demonstration.

ACCESS POINTS

Virtually all of the online catalogs available today provide searching by author, title and subject fields at the very least. Some provide a finer breakdown. For example, a user can stipulate whether the request is for a specific type of author—personal name, corporate name, conference name, etc. Similarly, some systems provide title access in the broad sense (i.e., including series titles, translated titles, etc.), while others require the user to indicate whether series title, uniform title or some other title is wanted.

The choice of access points depends to a large extent on the data base design and on how the various indexes have been constructed. Some systems provide access to the entire record with full keyword and Boolean logic available. This type of access is available only if the data base has an inverted file structure. Other systems, such as those that use derived search keys or phrase searching, are usually limited in the access points they can support to the ones that have been included in their indexes at the time the data base was constructed. (It is perhaps worth pointing out here the similarity between this approach to online access and the type of access available in the card catalog.)

In theory, there is no reason why the entire bibliographic citation cannot be accessible to users conducting online catalog searches. The decision to limit access to certain fields in some systems was made in the interests of conserving storage space and because designers thought they knew how users wanted to get information out of the catalog. (As discussed in Chapter 7, it became obvious from some of the earliest online catalog studies that users were doing far more subject searching than had been anticipated from similar studies in card catalogs.)

In some online catalogs, limiting search results to certain categories of materials (such as "English language" or " published since 1970") is accomplished by merely adding an additional specification to the retrieval criteria. In others (again, depending on the data base structure) the limiting factors must be applied after a set of citations is selected from the data base. Theoretically, there is no difference between an access point that is used for retrieval and one that is used for limiting search results. The difference lies only in how each has been implemented in a particular online catalog.

DISPLAY OPTIONS

As discussed in Chapter 3, some online catalog data bases have bibliographic records that are quite different from others. The CLSI system uses a brief record; the ILS system marketed by Avatar uses the full MARC record and preserves the MARC tagging structure; others fall somewhere between the two. Similarly, there is a variety of display options. Some provide a very brief record (such as call number and title) as the standard display, while others have as standard a record format that is reminiscent of the catalog card. Figure 6.3 shows a typical record display from the CLSI system and Figure 6.4 shows a full record display from the RLIN data base.

Which of these display formats is most appropriate, and whether more than one display format is needed, will depend to a large extent on the needs of the library's users. What is suitable for the children's room of the Springfield (VT) Town Library might be inappropriate at Yale, and vice versa. This is an area in which the library has quite a bit of latitude, since record displays can often be reformatted to suit the library's individual requirements. It must be remembered, however, that data base content may dictate display format: e.g., if the data base is composed of brief records, there is no way that full records can be produced from it.

Other available display options are: the ability to produce a printout on demand, the ability to sort the retrieved citations in some specified order, and the ability to view cita-

Figure 6.3: Sample Record Display on the CLSI System

```
CALL NUMB:    796.34/Brumfield
AUTHOR:       Brumfield, Charles
TITLE:        Off the wall: championship racquetball for the
              ardent amateur
PUBLISHER:    Dial Press, 1978
DESCRIPTION:  173 pages
SUBJECT1:     Racquetball
CALL NUMB:    796.34/Brumfield




       PUB    PUBYR    COST    MC    ED    L.A.D.

              *COPY INFORMATION FOLLOWS*

           IOC 3 1978 00127 6336 07/07/82



       START        BACK        PAGE        PAGE
       OVER         UP          BACK        NEXT        HELP
```

Figure 6.4: Sample Record Display on the RLIN System

```
PROD      Books       FUL/BIB    DCLC788031-B          Search          NHDG-OID
Cluster 5 of 8
+B
ID:DCLC788031-B      RTYP:c     ST:p    FRN:    NLR:       MS:p EL:   AD:04-18-78
CC:9110  BLT:am      DCF:i      CSC:    MOD:    SNR:       ATC:       UD:01-01-01
CP:nyu   L:eng       INT:       GPC:    BIO:    FIC:0      CON:
PC:s     PD:1978/               REP:    CPI:0   FSI:0      ILC:a    MEI:1   II:1
010      788031
020      0803772726.
020      0803772742 (pbk.)
040      ‡dCStRLIN
050 0    GV1017.R3‡bB78
082      796.34
100 10   Brumfield, Charles.
245 10   Off the wall :‡bchampionship racquetball for the ardent amateur /
    ‡cCharles Brumfield, Jeffrey Bairstow.
260 0    New York :‡bDial Press,‡c1978.
300      xi, 173 p. :‡bill. ;‡c26 cm.
500      Includes index.
650 0    Racquetball.
700 10   Bairstow, Jeffrey,‡d1939-‡ejoint author.
```

tions in brief or full form. The best way for a library to choose among these options is to see how they look in operation. Remember also that baud rate—the speed at which data are displayed at the terminal—is an important factor in user acceptance of one display format over another.

HARDWARE REQUIREMENTS

The computer hardware required by the various online catalog systems varies greatly. This is partly because of the wide range of libraries that must be accommodated, and partly for historical reasons. Computer systems developers tend to base new systems on equipment and procedures with which they are already familiar. Thus, it was quite natural, for example, for Northwestern University to use IBM equipment for its NOTIS and LUIS systems because IBM computers were already in widespread use on campus.

Some online catalogs run on only one kind of computer, such as Computer Cat on the Apple, while others run on any equipment that is compatible. Some online catalogs are based on transportable operating systems; that is, the operating system will run on more than one type of equipment. These are available in several different hardware configurations. Examples are NLM's Integrated Library System (ILS) and DataPhase's ALIS II, both of which use the MUMPS operating system. These online catalogs are available on Data General, DEC and Tandem equipment. CTI has two different versions of its online catalog—one that runs on Microdata minicomputers and one that runs on Prime computers. Despite the variations, there are some guidelines to keep in mind when evaluating different hardware configurations:

• Is the hardware all composed of standard "off-the-shelf" equipment? Is it brand new, or has it been around long enough to have accrued some sort of performance history?

• Who will maintain the equipment? Where is the nearest service center? What kind of realistic vendor response time can be expected?

• Is there any similar equipment nearby or available that could be used for backup?

• Are there knowledgeable people in the area who are familiar with the equipment? If some special features or other modifications are required, who will make them?

• Can the proposed computer hardware configuration be expanded if necessary?

The different terminals, printers and other online catalog components were already discussed in Chapter 4. These factors may, in some instances, be as important as the overall system differences, but they are usually given less weight because their cost is lower.

Finally, although having the right hardware is critical to the proper functioning of an online catalog, this consideration must always take second place to the software requirements. A system that operates perfectly but does the task inappropriately will never be satisfactory, but one that does the task well and hiccups occasionally may be forgiven its imperfections.

THE SELECTION PROCESS

The major steps that a library should follow when selecting an online catalog—and some pitfalls to avoid—are reviewed here. Chapter 5 discussed cost estimates, contract provisions and fund raising in more detail.

• Decide what the online catalog is supposed to do and whose needs it is intended to serve.

• Develop a list of requirements for the catalog. Understand the difference between *stating requirements* and giving design *specifications*. Stating the library's requirements completely and clearly will help guarantee that the system selected will perform as you wish.

• Contact several vendors to get information on the systems available.

• Estimate the probable costs and add 20%. Estimate the time needed. Double everything.

• Figure out how much money the library has to spend to start up and continue operation of the catalog. If these amounts are not large enough to cover the estimates generated above, stop any further work on procurement and start finding ways to raise the necessary money. It is unfair to send vendors a request for proposal when the library does not have the resources to purchase a system. If funds are available, the library can proceed with soliciting RFPs, choosing a vendor and negotiating the contract.

A FEW WARNINGS

As part of the selection process, a library should keep in mind the following warnings:

• Watch out for vendor promises to deliver software that does not now exist.

• Be skeptical of the "mockup demonstration." The danger signal sounds something like "Oh, this is just a demonstrator. The real system won't be ready to demonstrate until next..." Month? Year?

• Be wary of the need for special purpose hardware. If a vendor sugests that a special terminal (or some other device) will be needed that *does not now exist*, add at least two years to the schedule and plan for delays. Even special key caps take a very long time to make.

• Check with other libraries that have installed the system being contemplated (or one like it). See the system in operation if possible.

• Review the contract carefully, especially the payment schedule.

Finally, remember that the best online catalog system is the one that best meets the needs of the library installing it. There is no one "best" system for all circumstances. The library (or its patrons) will have to make the choice. If the library is honest about its needs and open in its dealings with vendors, the likelihood of success is very high. No one wants to see a system fail—least of all a vendor—so it is in everyone's interest to take steps to ensure a successful outcome.

7

Evaluating the Online Catalog

Because the online catalog is such a radical departure from its predecessors, evaluating its impact is especially important for the library. Assessment is difficult: there are still relatively few operational systems, and the ones that do exist have been in use for only a short time.

THE ONLINE PATRON ACCESS PROJECT

A nationwide Online Patron Access Project, sponsored by the Council on Library Resources (CLR), provided a great deal of useful information. The study was conducted between March and May 1982, and a summary of its results appeared in *Users Look at Online Catalogs*.[1] The Online Patron Access Project involved five participating organizations—the Library of Congress (LC), the Online Computer Library Center, Inc. (OCLC), the Research Libraries Group (RLG), J. Matthews and Associates, Inc. and the University of California—and 29 libraries with online catalog systems. The project was undertaken as a result of recommendations made at the 1980 Dartmouth Conference, discussed in Chapter 1.

The CLR project was designed to learn more about user perceptions of the online catalog and how patrons actually used it. Both users and non-users were queried. Appendix B shows the questionnaire for users. Appendix C shows the questionnaire for non-users. Readers should keep in mind that the survey results may have some bias, since the sample was not truly random.

---

1. Division of Library Automation and Library Research and Analysis Group, University of California at Berkeley, *Users Look at Online Catalogs: Results of a National Survey of Users and Non-users of Online Catalogs*, Final report to the Council on Library Resources, November 16, 1982.

MAJOR CONCLUSIONS OF THE CLR PROJECT

The first and perhaps most surprising finding of the Online Patron Access Project is that *people like online catalogs.* More than 90% of users surveyed had a favorable attitude toward the online catalog and an equal number responded that the computer catalog was better than the manual catalog. The finding holds for all user groups, types of libraries and computer catalogs included in the survey. Further, users like the online catalog whether they judge it independently or compare it to manual library catalogs.

Most users find out about the online catalog by noticing a terminal in the library. A high percentage of users reported that they learned to use the online catalog by themselves, without assistance from library staff members. A corollary of this finding is that patrons who are frequent users of the library are more likely to use the online catalog than patrons who use the library very rarely. More than 68.2% of online catalog users reported that they use their libraries at least once a week.

This finding also suggests that libraries should plan to locate terminals for the online catalog in highly visible places. Other responses indicate that providing enough terminals with plenty of space for writing and for stowing personal belongings is a very important part of user satisfaction with the system. In addition, users like the option of getting printed listings. Users also indicated that good signs and the availability of brochures and other material introducing the online catalog were beneficial.

Users of the online catalog consult it often; well over half use it on most of their visits to the library. But users of the online catalog also use the card catalog or other library catalogs on a regular basis.

WHO ARE THE USERS?

Online catalog users are not necessarily users of other computers or computer systems, according to the CLR study. For many users, the online catalog is the only computer system they have ever used, although an almost equal number use some other computer system at least once a week. However, users of the online catalog are more likely than non-users to have experience with some other computer system.

Online catalog users tend to be younger than non-users and men are more likely to be users than women. In addition, online catalog users tend to have more education than non-users.

In academic libraries, users come from all academic disciplines, but use is related to discipline. Those users who report that they are associated with the arts and humanities, interdisciplinary subjects and the social sciences are more likely to be users of the online catalog. Those in business, management, medical and health sciences, law, and those who have no major field of interest, are more likely to be non-users. Those in education and the physical and biological sciences have about the same proportion of users and non-users.

This division by discipline can probably be explained by the different types of library materials needed by users working in the various areas. For example, patrons working in the social sciences and humanities consult monographic materials extensively, while those working in the sciences make more use of journal literature and computer search aids. Since the content of most online catalogs is primarily monographic materials, and since none of the systems included in the study provides searching at the journal article level, the finding seems logical.

Reasons for Non-use

The reasons why some library patrons do not use the online catalog vary, but center on the response that the individual has not had time to learn how to use it. "Fear of computers" did not feature as an important factor in non-use.

Most non-users believe it will take less than 30 minutes to learn how to use the online catalog and that learning to use it will be easy. A majority of non-users believe that they will be able to learn to use the online catalog quickly, and almost three-quarters of them say that they are likely to use the online catalog in the future. The responses to the question of why some patrons do not use the online catalog are extremely ambiguous, and the authors of the report urge caution in interpreting the results.

Their conclusion is that the non-user is a person who is not a frequent user of the library or its catalogs. Yet these same non-users claim that they are likely to use the online catalog in the future and that it will be easy to learn. One implication of this seeming contradiction is that non-users may become users of the online catalog if their general library use increases. Another possible interpretation is that non-users, unsure of how to use the online catalog and perhaps a bit fearful of it, are reluctant to admit that fact.

Usage Related to Search Results

In general, as indicated above, users are very receptive to the online catalog, a response linked closely to satisfaction with search results. More than 80% of the users responded that they found at least something that was relevant to their search request, and those who got more than they were looking for were very favorably disposed toward the online catalog.

Frequent users of the online catalog were generally more satisfied with the search results than were patrons who used it rarely. This corresponds with the finding that users who are familiar with the online catalog tend to retrieve more material. On the other hand, users who retrieve nothing of value tend rather quickly to become non-users.

Almost half of the online catalog users reported that they discovered materials of interest that they were not looking for. Serendipity does seem to have an effect on user satisfaction. Almost 60% of users who rated their search as "very satisfactory" also reported that they accidentally found items of interest.

In addition, the following findings emerged from the study regarding the effects of subject searching on user satisfaction:

- The easier it is to do subject searching, the more relevant material is retrieved.

- Easy subject searching improves search satisfaction.

- When subject searching is easy, users are more likely to come across other things of interest.

- Subject searching problems have an important effect on overall attitude toward the online catalog.

USER PROBLEMS

The survey attempted to get information on the kinds of difficulties that users of online catalogs may have. These include:

- Knowing what materials are included in the online catalog;

- Increasing or decreasing the number of items when too few or too many are retrieved;

- Knowing how to search with truncated terms;

- Knowing the correct subject term;

- Scanning through a long display (forward or backward);

- Interrupting or stopping the display;

- Entering commands at any time during the search process;

- Remembering the sequence or order of commands;

- Using logical operators such as AND, OR and NOT;

- Using codes or abbreviations for searching;

- Understanding abbreviations on the screen;

- Searching by call number;

- Searching by subject;

- Finding that response time is too slow;

- Finding that selecting from a list of choices takes too much time;

- Entering exact spelling, initials, spaces and hyphens;

- Retrieving messages that are too long (i.e., give more information than is needed);

- Understanding the initial instructions.

USER SUGGESTIONS

Users were asked to specify improvements to the online catalog. They were asked to select from a list of features ranging from system enhancements to changes in the library environment surrounding the online catalog.

System Enhancements

The following, ranked in order of frequency of response, are the online catalog system modifications that users most often requested.

- Ability to view a list of words related to the search terms used;

- Ability to search a book's table of contents, summary or index;

- Ability to know if a book is checked out;

- Ability to print search results;

- Ability to search by any word or words in a subject heading;

- Provision of step-by-step instructions;

- Ability to search for illustrations and bibliographies;

- Ability to tell where a book is located in the library;

- Ability to change the order in which the items are displayed;

- Ability to limit search results by date of publication and language;

- Ability to search by call number.

While some of these features are available in some of the systems included in the survey, the list still illustrates the importance users attach to various systems features that they think should be available.

Data Base Enhancements

Users were also asked to select the additional kinds of materials they would like included in the online catalog data base. The responses, again ranked in order of frequency, are:

- Newspapers;

- Government publications;

- More of the library's older books;

- Journals/magazines;

- Dissertations;

- Phonograph records or tapes;

- Technical reports;

- Motion picture films;

- Maps;

- Manuscripts;

- Music scores.

Of course, these are based on aggregate figures for all the libraries included in the survey. In libraries that do not include one of the top four categories of items in the data base, the priority for adding that item type rises to first place.

Environmental Improvements

Online catalog users were also asked to rank library service improvements that would enhance their use of the system. The choice of responses fell into two broad categories: 1) number and location of terminals, and 2) availability and type of information or instruction. Users said (as expected) that they wanted more terminals both in and outside the library. Their preferred source of information on how to use the online catalog was a chart of commands posted at the terminal. The second preferred source of information was a manual or brochure at the terminal. Training sessions and audiovisual programs were lower on the list. Fewer than 10% of users indicated that they would like an instruction manual for purchase.

PLANNING ADVICE FOR LIBRARY MANAGERS

The online patron access survey also presented some suggestions for library administrators who may be considering installation of an online catalog. The major findings are:

Fears that an online catalog will have a negative effect on users or on library service are unjustified. The evidence shows that users are very happy with the online catalog, and that even those who have not yet tried it have a generally favorable attitude toward it. Although it is certainly true that some online catalogs provide a higher degree of user satisfaction than others, users prefer the online catalog to the catalog forms it replaces regardless of the quality of the online product.

Make the online catalog visible. Put the terminals where library patrons can't help seeing them. The evidence shows that the online catalog sells itself to users who find out about it. Furthermore, patrons who use the online catalog tend to continue using it on subsequent library visits.

Promote the use of the library and the online catalog will promote itself. The evidence shows that online catalog users find out about it by seeing the terminals in the library. They learn to use it with the help of printed and online aids. Most non-users are also non-users or infrequent users of the library and other library catalogs. Therefore, the implication is that to encourage online catalog use, it is necessary to encourage library use.

Plan for a lot of terminals. Since users said that they wanted more terminals, administrators should not think in terms of a single location near the card catalog. How many terminals are enough is difficult to answer. "As many as you can afford!" usually turns out to be as accurate as any other estimate.

Plan for lots of wiring. Before terminals can be installed, the necessary telecommunications facilities must be provided. Ten times as much as you think you need now will probably not be enough.

Provide lots of writing space at the terminal. Many users complained that there was inadequate space at the terminals for their belongings and papers.

Provide printers. Many users said that they would like to have printouts of their search results. Further, it is inefficient use of online catalog time to have users taking notes from the terminal screen when they could get a quick printout to take with them. The printers must be easy to use. Users should be able to add more paper if necessary, and there should be someone on call to assist with any problems.

Provide more and better printed aids. Most online catalog users learn to use the online catalog from printed sources and most turn to guides or brochures when they need help. Brief guides, available at the terminals, are preferred.

Provide online assistance. Good online instruction alleviates the need for both printed aids and staff assistance. But the evidence shows that halfway measures just won't do. Poorly thought-out help screens and instructions may just confuse users and add to their reliance on help from public service staff.

To improve user satisfaction, improve the system not the training. Survey findings show that the best way to improve user satisfaction is not to teach users how to deal with the system's inadequacies, but to fix the system.

Plan for better subject access. Much of the survey data indicate a close link between user satisfaction and success in conducting subject searches. The following are two ways in which this can be achieved.

First, make subject searching easier. "Finding the correct subject term" was among the most serious problems that users have with the online catalog. The best solution to this problem is to provide free-text searching throughout the entire bibliographic citation. This will enable the user to conduct subject searches using the terminology that comes to mind, rather than being limited by the artificialities introduced by controlled vocabularies. Another way of simplifying subject searching is to provide cross-reference information for various headings. This allows users to look at terms that are related to the search terms they have in mind.

A second way to provide better subject access is to provide more in-depth indexing for the items in the online catalog. A frequently cited improvement desired by users was the "ability to search a book's table of contents, summary or index." This finding implies that users do not consider the few subject headings that are now commonly assigned to items during cataloging adequate for determining the content of materials. Cochrane and others have been advocating enriched subject access for a long time, and now it appears that online catalog users are clearly stating that need as well.[2]

Plan to enlarge the data base. Many users want additional materials included in the online catalog. Not only are older materials wanted, but items in other formats, such as maps and phonograph records, are highly desirable. One of the first happy users at the Dartmouth College Library was heard to exclaim "Hey, this is great! Now what do I have to do to use this terminal to search for journal articles and newspapers?"

This remark and some of the other conclusions about user attitudes indicate that the real problem facing libraries as they install online catalog systems is not how to convince patrons to use them, but how to keep one step ahead of their rising expectations and demands.

TECHNICAL QUESTIONS REMAINING

Although the Online Patron Access Project provided excellent information on user perceptions of the online catalog and their use of it, a number of more technical questions remain unanswered. Some of these are:

• Would a search in an online catalog and its manual counterpart show comparable recall and relevance figures? If they are different, how are they different? Do the differences depend on the nature of the inquiry?

• Does it take more or less time to conduct a search using the online catalog than a comparable search in a card catalog? If there are differences, do they depend on the nature of the inquiry?

2. Pauline A. Cochrane, "Subject Access in the Online Catalog," *Research Libraries in OCLC,* 5 (January 1982): 1-7.

• Are there any types of information that are difficult or impossible to locate in the online catalog? If so, which? Why?

• Do some types of searches take much longer than others? If so, which? Why?

• What search features are most effective in producing good results (i.e., high relevance, high recall)?

• In those online catalogs that provide a variety of search features, such as keyword searching, Boolean operators, truncation and so forth, which are most often used? Least used? Why?

• What techniques work best for broadening a search that is too narrow?

• What techniques work best for narrowing a search that is too general?

• What limiting or other qualifying features are the most useful?

• What display formats and features do patrons like best? Are some formats only used by the library staff?

• What user interface mode (or modes) works best? Is baud rate a factor?

• Do users prefer full-face or line-by-line mode terminals? Do they care?

LISTEN TO USERS

Libraries can collect a lot of valuable information from users of the online catalog by interviewing them as they complete their searches. Most people are very happy to share their reactions and ideas with library staff—especially if they think the online catalog is still experimental and they have a chance to influence its design. Although to a certain extent user reactions tend to polarize around the "I think it's great" or "I think it stinks" extremes, users are able to articulate quite nicely what they specifically like and don't like. The following user comments from the CLR survey are representative.

"Need to systematize a way to locate the exact journal needed when you don't know the title."

"The commands are easy to type in and correct."

"Too verbose, but much needed and welcomed."

"Need more cross-references—I like it though!"

"Terminals go down too often, or refuse to spit out information."

"I wish it [was] easier to stop the computer terminal at a certain point."

"Finding the item in a long list takes too much time."

"Use of the terminal is a hit-or-miss proposition if you don't know the date of publication. In this regard, the card catalog is probably quicker."

"The commands on the screen are easy, but remembering not to type 'a' for title and vice versa is difficult."

"[I] was frustrated when I knew only [the] subject, instead of title/author."

"Long lists should be in alphabetical sequence for easier retrieval."

"Listing too slow. Need higher baud rate; should have brief mode that talks less to user."

"Author search is difficult when an author is listed by the proper name but not by the pseudonym."

"I think the search should give reasons for failure to find the book of interest."

"Please make available a display of all subjects using alphabetical listings."

"I like it, but get an English-only option on the search—and a chair!"

"You should be able to go backward and forward between search displays."

"Displayed messages take too long and should be interruptible."

"[The] log-in message gets tedious after 50 times!"

As can be seen from these examples, library users are able to recommend ways to make online catalog systems better. The most important thing for librarians and others who are interested in the future of online catalogs to do now is to *pay attention to what users have to say.* In an article discussing the characteristics of online catalogs Stephen R. Salmon commented, "Librarians have been trying for centuries to help users find what they want, and online catalogs provide a major step forward in doing this. Our challenge now is to use this tool and refine it, so that our services rise to a new and higher level." [3]

THE OPPORTUNITY FOR LIBRARIES

In order to meet this challenge, however, we must be able to admit that we don't know all the answers. For centuries librarians have codified, classified, organized and indexed materials to make it easier for users to get the information they needed. Although these

3. Stephen R. Salmon, "Characteristics of Online Catalogs," *Library Resources and Technical Services* 27 (1) (January/March 1983): 36-67.

structures made it easier for the library to maintain its collections, in some cases it became a question of whose interests were primarily being served: the library's or its users'.

Because the online catalog is an entirely new product, it gives the library a rare opportunity to let the users have a hand in deciding what the online catalog should do and how it should work. None of the online catalogs now operational in this country is more than 10 years old. Therefore, there are no long traditions to be overcome, no firmly entrenched sets of procedures, rules and ideas about how things ought to be done that must be changed before any progress can be made. The whole field is so new that if we had to throw everything out—all the systems that have been built in the last decade—and start afresh, the loss would not be catastrophic.

What we have instead is a tremendous opportunity to produce a tool that is designed to be used, that meets public need, that lets users tell us what *they* want for a change. Further, the technical resources are finally available to build almost anything the public can ask for. Therefore, as plans are being made to install more and more online catalogs in libraries throughout the world, we have an obligation to ask some hard, evaluative questions about the new systems and to listen to patrons as they adapt to the new technology.

Value of the User's Perspective

Precisely because library users are not trained librarians, are not familiar with cataloging and filing rules, and do not necessarily know all about Library of Congress Subject Headings, they can tell us a great deal about what they need to get information. Further, because many of the library's users have no formal training in computer science, they have no preconceived notions about what can and cannot be done. Thus freed from both sets of rigorous rules, procedures and protocols, library users can tell us what they would *like* the online catalog to do. Librarians (and systems designers) must be prepared for the harsh reality that this may differ greatly from our assumptions about how users will want to access information. Then we must have the courage to go ahead and build what patrons want and discard many of our notions about how things ought to be done.

Integrating User Needs and Library Tradition

This, of course, does not mean that the library has to reject all its time-honored procedures for cataloging materials and organizing information. Rather, it means that librarians must recognize that while those techniques may have worked well for the library, they may not have been as beneficial for users. We will have to understand that the library can be flexible, that it does not have to abide by one set of rules and procedures for everybody, that it is perfectly all right for information to be stored in one way and retrieved in another. The important thing is the end result: *that the library's users get the information they seek.*

GUIDELINES FOR IMPROVING AND EVALUATING THE CATALOG

With this objective in mind, here are some suggestions for improving the online catalog and for determining if the new systems are successful:

- Provide the online catalog with a built-in suggestion box or online mail file so that users can easily register their comments, suggestions and ideas. Have someone respond to each of these.

- Have a resource person on hand to answer questions from users. This person—a professional staff member—must be a knowledgeable reference librarian as well as a trained searcher, and must also have some knowledge of the workings of the online catalog system.

- Keep transaction logs of user sessions with the online catalog. It has been noted that there is a discrepancy between what users report they are doing at the terminal and what they are actually doing. Without in any way infringing on users' privacy, much valuable information can be collected on how they are interacting with the system.

- Interview users at the terminal. Find out what kind of problems they are having. Get comments on how the system can be improved.

- Don't rule out *any* user suggestion because it seems implausible. Many commonplace online catalog search features were undreamed of 30 years ago. At the rate at which new technology is forthcoming, no user suggestion should be ignored simply because the technology to support it doesn't exist today.

- Conduct some carefully controlled comparative tests of the online catalog and the card catalog. These tests will provide a baseline for comparison of future system enhancements.

- Individual libraries should plan for periodic formal evaluations of the online catalog. In addition, a nationwide survey, such as the Online Patron Access Project, should be conducted from time to time.

- In addition to evaluating the online catalog, the library should also evaluate the effectiveness of its signs and brochures, orientation programs, training programs, etc.

- Involve the library staff. Librarians' ideas and requirements may be far too stringent for the typical library user, but staff members are the resource of last resort for many patrons. Consequently, while the online catalog may not need a high level of discriminatory capability most of the time, the additional systems features needed to meet librarians' requirements may be extremely useful in cases that are too complex for the user to handle unassisted.

- Since frequent library users tend to be users of the online catalog, the library should examine its public relations programs occasionally to see if they are encouraging general library use.

- Finally, the library should ask its users what other related services it could provide that would enhance users' access to information. Some possible enhancements to the online catalog might be online access to the various bibliographic utilities, online access to some publications that are available only in machine-readable form, word processing or other information processing services.

By monitoring user acceptance of its services and by conducting evaluation programs from time to time, the library can maintain its awareness of user needs and priorities. By continually assessing the value of its services and by remaining open to the needs of its users, the library can remain responsive to its patrons and keep up with the headlong rush into the Information Age.

8

The Integrated Library System

The online catalog, important as it is, is just one component of a group of systems that exist in any library. In fact, many vendors of online catalogs do not market them separately, but sell the online catalog as one part of a total package. The functions that are usually supported in such packages are:

- Reference services (the online catalog);

- Acquisitions;

- Cataloging;

- Serials receipt;

- Binding;

- Interlibrary loan;

- Circulation; and

- Materials booking.

All of these systems taken together and considered as one are usually described as an *integrated library system* or a *total integrated library system*. Such a system is usually the goal, the *sine qua non*, of library automation. The situation in libraries today is somewhat analogous to the situation in the corporate environment some years ago when everyone was proclaiming the virtues of the "totally integrated management information system." After the initial euphoria wore off, people found that such systems were extremely difficult to define, almost impossible to build, extraordinarily costly and not necessarily the panacea that had been envisioned.

Libraries today face the danger of falling into the same trap. While an integrated system might be right for some libraries now or in the near future, it may represent unrealistic, pie-in-the-sky thinking for others. It is important for each institution to examine very closely its reasons for automating any function and to realize that it has the options of full automation, partial automation or no automation at all.

Since many libraries will, in fact, consider an online catalog as part of a total integrated system, this chapter will briefly discuss all the functions that might be candidates for automation.

CRITERIA FOR AUTOMATION

It is important to keep the following general caveats in mind when considering whether or not to automate:

• A good manual system is almost invariably better than a haphazardly implemented automated system.

• Merely putting a function on the computer or "online" will not clean up a poorly thought-out procedure. In fact, it will probably make it worse.

• Not every task worth doing is worth automating.

• Automation almost never eliminates any jobs or saves any money. It may change the kinds of tasks that people need to do, but rarely if ever does it actually decrease the number of people needed to do them. Similarly, it may change the way in which funds are allocated, but it seldom reduces the actual dollar expenditures.

Before automating any particular library function, the following questions should be asked:

• Is there considerable repetitive work involved?

• Are 80% to 90% of the transactions or operations to be performed perfectly straight-forward and regular, requiring little thought and almost no decision making?

• How important are the exceptions? Can the exceptions be grouped into a small number of easily defined special cases? What about the exceptions to those?

• Is speed important? Accuracy? Record-keeping?

• Why does automating this function seem attractive? Is is merely "the thing to do" or will it truly solve some problem?

• What will happen if the function is not automated?

Let us examine each of the library systems mentioned above in the light of these criteria.

REFERENCE SERVICES: THE ONLINE CATALOG

The conventional library card catalog is a triumph of intellectual organization. Although entirely manual, it is a real-time, random access retrieval device that allows patrons to get information about the library's holdings. It provides cross-references and other guides to its use, and it attempts to pull related materials together under the same headings. Its major shortcomings are:

- It is available only in the library.

- The patron must be familiar with library cataloging practice in order to use it effectively.

- Access points to the information contained in the bibliographic records are extremely limited. Because of the enormous work involved in assigning and maintaining added entries, the number of access points is not likely to grow.

- The card catalog gradually becomes inconsistent because of changes in cataloging practice, changes in terminology, changes in filing rules and so forth.

Reasons for Automating the Catalog

As noted previously, for a relatively small library collection (under 10,000 items), a conventional card catalog may be perfectly adequate. In fact, for small collections, patrons may not really need a catalog at all—browsing through the collection may be a far more effective method of finding out what is in the library. Some user studies have shown that in smaller libraries few if any patrons consult the card catalog; they prefer to go directly to the stacks. Access to large collections is generally helped by having some sort of catalog. Providing good access to very large collections is probably impossible without an online catalog.

The minimum size library collection for which an online catalog would be cost-effective is difficult to state absolutely. Other factors besides the number of items must be considered. Some are:

- The nature and anticipated use of the collection. For example, a corporate library with 10,000 technical reports might benefit from online access while a public library with 10,000 volumes might manage quite well with a manual system.

- The need for remote access to the bibliographic citations.

- Whether a machine-readable catalog is needed for other purposes.

- What, if any, computer support is available.

Integrating the Online Catalog Data Base with Other Functions

One of these factors—whether a machine-readable catalog is needed for other purposes—may overshadow all the others. Although the library can be envisioned as a group of more or less separate but interlocking systems, the collection of bibliographic information that comprises the library's catalog may be central to most of them.

In fact, some integrated library systems are organized so that the online catalog data base forms the heart of the entire operation. Figure 8.1 shows the plan of the integrated library system developed by the Lister Hill National Center for Biomedical Communications at the National Library of Medicine.[1] An integrated bibliographic data base forms the core of the system and each of the separate subsystems uses it.

Figure 8.2 shows a different representation of an integrated library system—one which is perhaps more realistic in terms of data base creation and maintenance. In this plan, the online catalog data base contains *only* the bibliographic citations (with perhaps a bar code number and a bibliographic utility identification number). Other information needed by the various subsystems is stored in auxiliary files.

Figure 8.1: The Integrated Library System at the National Library of Medicine

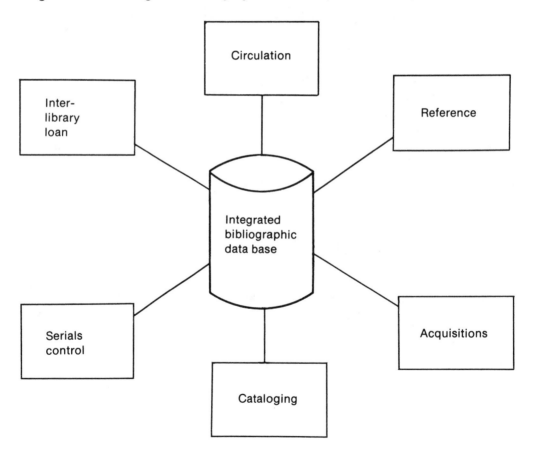

1. Lister Hill National Center for Biomedical Communications, National Library of Medicine, "The Integrated Library System: Overview and Status " (Bethesda, MD: October 1979).

Figure 8.2: A Plan for an Integrated Library System

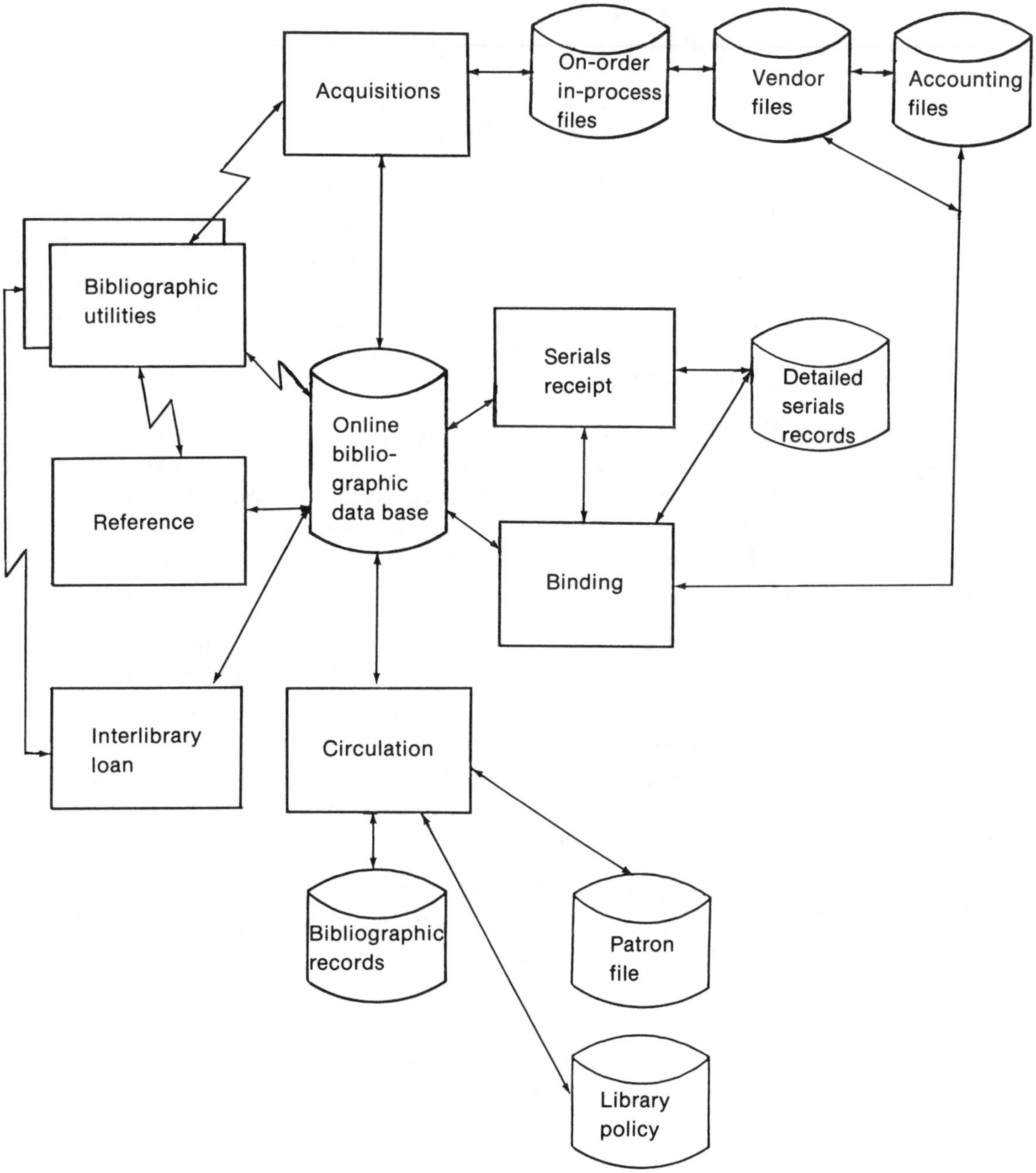

This plan requires only that the online catalog data base be accessible to each of the major functions. It does not require the central data base to contain all the information needed to support each function. Note also that the circulation system in this plan has its own data base, which is distinct from the online catalog. This is because a library may need to keep circulation information for items that are not in its catalog; for example, individual periodical issues, parts of multiple-volume monographic sets, ephemera, reprints on reserve or personal copies.

ACQUISITIONS

Acquisitions services deal with adding items to the library's collection by purchase, exchange or gift. Much of the work is repetitive. Once the decision to order an item has been made and a vendor selected, the next step is to place an order for the item and wait for it to come in. If the item does not arrive, a reminder is sent to the vendor (claiming), and if the money used to purchase the item must be accounted for, some means of recording the price paid is needed. Speed, accuracy and record-keeping are required—all attributes of computer-supported systems.

Acquisitions, then, is a very likely function to automate in a library. The big question to answer before proceeding is whether the library places enough orders each year to justify the cost of automating. If the answer is "no," there is no shame in continuing to support acquisitions with a good manual system. On the other hand, new microcomputer-based acquisitions systems make automated acquisitions systems affordable to much smaller libraries than in the past.

An example is the Innovacq 100 system available from Innovative Interfaces, Inc. This system enables library staff to search on-order or in-process files; to create new bibliographic records either by direct keyboard entry or by interfacing with a bibliographic utility; to update records; to produce orders, claim notices, cancellations and so forth; and to view each record online. Because it is a stand-alone system (although it can be linked with a bibliographic utility), Innovacq 100 makes it quite possible for a library to automate just the acquisitions operation and at a cost that is not prohibitive.

For larger libraries, there are a number of vendors that offer integrated library systems that include acquisitions. Among them are CTI Library Systems, Inc., Avatar Systems, Inc., Data Research Associates and Biblio-Techniques, Inc.

CATALOGING

Because of the high cost of cataloging library materials, the cooperative cataloging systems were among the first automated library systems to be devised. The bibliographic utilities OCLC and the Research Libraries Group's Research Libraries Information Network (RLIN) are the two largest and best-known, but there are others. A few libraries such as the Northwestern University Library and the National Library of Medicine have developed their own online cataloging systems. (It must be remembered that an *online catalog* and *online cataloging* are not the same thing. Online cataloging creates the bibliographic records in an online environment; the online catalog provides a method for searching those records online.)

Almost any library—large or small—can benefit from cooperative online cataloging. A library can join a regional service such as the New England Library Information Network (NELINET), the Southeastern Library Network, Inc. (SOLINET) or the Washington Library Network (WLN), or it may receive cataloging information from a vendor such as Blackwell North America, Inc., Gaylord Bros., Inc. or Brodart, Inc. Many libraries have chosen to begin their library automation effort with online cataloging because the savings to the library are so great and the investment in systems and equipment is so small.

Automating the cataloging function also gives the library a start at building a machine-readable data base that can be used to automate other functions. The bibliographic citations produced by cataloging are generally available to the library on magnetic tape or may even be transmitted online from the bibliographic utility. Further, a bibliographic utility usually does not restrict a library's use of the cataloging records produced, providing they are not resold in some form.

Avatar Systems, Inc., the Northwestern University Library, Data Research Associates and the University of Toronto are among the vendors that offer online catalog systems that support online cataloging.

SERIALS RECEIPT

Library patrons generally would like to know not only if the library subscribes to a particular periodical, but whether or not a specific issue has been received. In addition, the library staff itself needs this information in order to claim missing issues. Libraries have traditionally used manual card files to keep track of this information. Where regular publications are involved, these files usually meet the needs of the staff quite well. They are always available; they can be accessed at random; they can be varied to suit exceptional cases; and they are relatively fast and easy to use. The major drawbacks of these manual systems are that they are not available to the library user and they provide no automatic way of detecting missing issues or alerting the library when an item should be claimed, which makes it especially difficult to keep track of irregular publications.

Successful automated serials receipt systems have been "just around the corner" for at least 10 years. Some of the early efforts are perhaps classic examples of computerization gone awry. The main problem with serials receipt control is that despite the repetitive and clerical nature of the work involved, the whole procedure is shot through with all sorts of exceptions and irregularities which inevitably bog down any computerized system. First of all, there are at least a dozen "standard" frequencies of publication:

- Daily;

- Daily except Sunday;

- Weekly;

- Semi-weekly;

- Biweekly;

- Monthly;

- Semi-monthly;

- Bimonthly;

- Quarterly;

- Once every four months;

- Annual;

- Semiannual.

In addition to these, there are the "weekly, 51 weeks per year" and the "monthly except July and August" variations. Then there are those regular publications which from time to time publish special issues that fall outside the normal pattern. There are so many exceptional cases that, as a result, no automated system developed to date does the job very well.

Before attempting to automate the serials receipt control function, a library should consider whether introducing a computer into the process is going to solve problems or introduce problems that do not exist with the more primitive, but flexible, manual systems of the past. Unquestionably, for a small library, a manual system will be far more cost-effective. A large library, which receives many thousands of titles and which retains bound issues, may need to consider an automated system to aid the claiming and binding processes and to provide users with detailed holdings information. Nevertheless, until more work is done in this area, serials receipt control remains one of those library functions which may best be left un-automated, and any library considering automation on this task should look over the alternatives very carefully.

Most vendors are just now developing serials receipt control systems for inclusion in their integrated systems. Some who are quite well along in this work are Avatar, CTI and Data Research Associates.

BINDING

Determining when a complete serials volume is ready to be bound and how to bind it is another of those functions that may best be left un-automated. There are so many variables involved in deciding what to bind and how and when to bind it that a computer-based serials binding control system may introduce more problems than it eliminates. A desirable alternative is to indicate through the serials receipt control system when a volume has been completed or when issues are missing. In addition, an online circulation system might contain information that would tell patrons when particular items are at the bindery.

INTERLIBRARY LOAN

Interlibrary loan is often thought of as a reference service activity. However, because it is an example (like cataloging) of a case where a library may want to be connected to another library's online catalog or to a central online data base, it is worth discussing briefly on its own.

Interlibrary loan is the time-honored method of providing patrons with materials that are not available in the library's own collections. The library may have access to a local, regional, statewide or national union catalog of library holdings. Most interlibrary loan requests begin with a search of the union catalog to determine if the desired item is held by any library and if it is available for loan. Once a source is identified, the request is sent to the appropriate library and the item is then forwarded to the patron.

As all librarians know, this process is time-consuming and expensive. Online access to a union catalog data base can change the interlibrary loan process dramatically by simplifying and speeding up the entire procedure. Further, control of loaned items is likely to be better if a computer can be used to keep track of their whereabouts. A well-functioning interlibrary loan system can also help a library control acquisitions costs by enabling libraries within a loaning group to share the more expensive materials.

Interlibrary loan is one of the best functions for a library to automate. The investment in hardware is usually limited to a terminal, a modem, and phone line or a dedicated line. The improved service usually quickly offsets the small additional cost. In addition, libraries sharing the online catalog data base for interlibrary loan may be able to use the data base to automate other library operations.

CIRCULATION

Automating the circulation system is perhaps the one most dramatic change the library can make in its daily operation. Although from a systems standpoint the automated circulation system operation is virtually identical to the manual system, to the patron the whole operation looks different because of the terminals, light pens and other equipment involved. An automated circulation system can also provide improved management information, such as which items in the collection circulate. This type of information is valuable for determining patron interests, for guiding acquisitions and for deciding which volumes should be sent to a remote storage site.

There are many variables to consider when making a decision on whether or not to automate circulation. These include the size of the collection, the size of the community served, the number of actual users, the volume of circulation transactions and the volume of overdue notices and other reports. Economies of scale are also a major factor. Some very small libraries can use a microcomputer-based circulation system, requiring only a small investment in computer equipment. Still others may be able to use a time-shared system in conjunction with other libraries, while large libraries may need to purchase or develop a system tailored to their needs.

There are many excellent guides for libraries contemplating the installation of an online circulation system.[2] These provide good information for any library seeking to install an online circulation system. In passing, however, we should point out that several of these systems claim to incorporate an online catalog function as well. Although some of the systems do indeed allow a user to query the data base in a limited fashion, few of the systems qualify as online catalogs according to the definition proposed in this book. On the other hand, almost all of the online catalogs offered have circulation system support as well. (The bibliographic utilities do not have a circulation system component at present.)

Among the vendors offering online catalogs with circulation system support are the Claremont Colleges Library, CLSI, DataPhase Systems, Inc. and Geac Canada Ltd.

MATERIALS BOOKING

Some integrated systems have a subsystem that assists the library in scheduling the loan or use of films, film projectors, slides, conference rooms and the like. Two vendors that provide this capability are DataPhase Systems, Inc. and Data Research Associates.

DEFINING NEEDS AND REQUIREMENTS

The most important thing a library must do in deciding whether to install an online catalog or any other automated library system is to identify its requirements as thoroughly and precisely as possible. There are few if any guidelines that might assist a library in accomplishing this task. We often assume that anyone knowledgeable about libraries and computers ought to be able to say what is needed. But it turns out that determining requirements and writing specifications is one of the most difficult parts of automating any function. According to an article in *Datamation*, "One of the most common reasons systems fail is because the definition of system requirements is bad."[3] This article is mandatory reading for any library that is seriously considering using a computer to do anything, including putting up an online catalog.

Being aware of the potential pitfalls, recognizing the parts of the requirements analysis that can *only* be done by the library staff and understanding the kind of information that is needed to design a good system will enable the library to make sound decisions about automating any of its operations. The same considerations will be necessary for evaluating integrated library systems, which are sure to proliferate.

The following chapter examines other issues which will have a bearing on library operations and online catalogs in the future.

---

2. See, for example, Joseph R. Matthews, *Comparative Information for Automated Circulation Systems* (Grass Valley, CA: 1981).
3. Laura Sharer, "Pinpointing Requirements," *Datamation* 27 (4) (April 1981): 139 ff.

9

The Online Catalog in the Information Age

The online public access catalog is just one manifestation of the massive changes that are taking place as we plunge into the Information Age. Another, which has been receiving more and more attention in recent years, is electronic publishing. The relationship between these two phenomena, and their implications for libraries, will be explored briefly here.

ONLINE ACCESS AND ELECTRONIC PUBLISHING

For some time now, advances in computer technology have been changing the traditional modes of publishing. Laboriously typed manuscripts, hand-set type and old-fashioned printing presses have been gradually replaced by methods that use word processors, photocomposition and other new forms of typesetting, all of which can convert text into machine-readable form.

Initially, only the publishing process was affected; the end products—books, magazines, newspapers—retained their traditional forms. However, as computer technology has become more sophisticated and affordable, and as the costs of printed products and traditional delivery methods continue to rise, publishers and other information providers have become increasingly interested in delivering their products in electronic form.

It is not surprising that libraries, already awash in a flood of journals and other printed matter, and caught in an economic crunch, might view electronic publishing as the hope of the future. In fact, many see the online public access catalog as the first step in the evolution of the library in a "paperless society."

Implications for Patrons and Libraries

Ideally, online publishing coupled with online public access in libraries could solve several large problems in one masterstroke:

- It could relieve some of the storage problems that libraries face in the wake of the information explosion. Libraries can no longer afford to construct ever-larger buildings to hold their mushrooming collections. Even the use of high density shelving and remote storage facilities are only temporary measures. At Dartmouth alone, the library's collection has doubled in size every 40 years since the founding of the college, and every 20 years since 1900! There is no way that Dartmouth can cope with this flood of information without making some materials available only in remote data bases.

- It could give patrons in even the smallest and most remote libraries timely access to the world's information. Currently, if materials are not available through interlibrary loan (which can be a time-consuming process), scholars and researchers must travel to metropolitan areas in order to use the large library collections often available there and nowhere else. Online access will make these large collections as close as the nearest terminal. Patrons will be able to obtain copies of any material they need easily and quickly.

- Library users could pursue their interests across disciplines, types of materials and geographic locations. Furthermore, having the actual text of many materials available online would finally allow users to find information, rather than find locators to materials that may or may not contain the information being sought. This, more than any other single factor, will revolutionize the way people do research.

There are further implications for libraries:

- Although print publications are unlikely to disappear, more and more materials—especially directories and periodicals—will be in electronic formats. The newspaper we have all come to know and love with our morning coffee may someday be replaced by a VDT, and the stacks of journals in our libraries may be replaced by rows of public access terminals.

- Libraries will have access to online information sources, so that patrons can get information on a wide range of topics. Users will be able to browse through electronic newspapers, magazines and other once-traditional library materials, as well as consult the local events bulletin board, get shopping advice and see the latest local restaurant menus.

- More and more libraries may create interest profiles of frequent library users in order to have items reflecting users' interests on hand.

- Libraries will include even more audio cassettes, video cassettes, floppy disks, video discs, computer software and other non-print items in their collections. Patrons will be able to check these items out for use as they would any other items. Some libraries already have successful computer lending programs whereby patrons check out microcomputers for home use.

- Libraries will be able to provide, on-demand, hard (printed) copies of many items that are not available in the library.

- Libraries will have to promote their services more heavily, in order to make users aware of all the various sources of information available. Users will have many options—a book, an article, computer program or video disc—all containing the information they need.

- Reference librarians will *not* be out of a job. Library users will be able to answer some questions themselves, but the library staff will still get many difficult, interesting, challenging queries.

- Many users will still want the library to "do it" for them. The situation has been likened to the introduction of the home permanent. For $1.25, women could give themselves a "salon quality" permanent wave at home, and beauty parlors all over the country were afraid that these products would ruin their business. Did it happen? No! People still like to be waited on, and they are still happy to have someone else do something they think is too technical, too hard or too much trouble.

- The library will still be very much in demand and librarians will still be needed to help patrons find their way around the system. One hopes that the task will be easier using online access and that some of the tedious aspects of reference work will be eliminated by the great power of online searching.

Obstacles to Electronic Information Delivery

There is no question that, properly implemented, electronic publishing and online public access combined could improve the amount and quality of the information available to patrons, and could help solve the problem of how libraries can store materials that are increasing almost exponentially. However, several major issues remain to be resolved, some of which are already the subject of raging controversy. It is beyond the scope of this book to discuss these issues in detail, but the main points are summarized below.

- Costs. Who will pay for these services? If the library charges for them, what will be the impact of online access on people's right to know? How will those who cannot afford even the simplest terminal fare in this electronic world? What is the library's responsibility in this area? What services should be provided free? For those that cannot be provided without cost, who pays and how much?

- Copyright. Who owns the data? How will authors and publishers be protected? How will libraries be protected? What constitutes "fair use?" Further, who will pay for the information, and how will such charges be implemented? Today, users of Dialog, Bibliographic Retrieval Services (BRS) and other utilities are charged a fee to search the data bases and a fee for copies of individual records. However, "downloading" (copying) of data bases without reimbursement to the data base producer is becoming a prevalent practice and a major concern of data base producers. This issue surfaced in December 1982, when the Online Computer Library Center (OCLC) copyrighted its data base—a decision which seems destined to be tested in court.

- Privacy. Who has a right to access which data? Does anyone have the right to monitor who is accessing which data files? Does the need to keep records to bill properly for services provided constitute an invasion of privacy? If patrons have interest profiles stored in their libraries, who may change or have access to them? What patron information can be collected in connection with the operation of an online catalog or circulation system that does not violate user privacy? Can demographic information be collected if given voluntarily?

THE ONLINE CATALOG: LIBRARY OF THE FUTURE

As for the online catalog, in the future it will not be discussed as a separate entity except by technicians. Rather, the online catalog will be just one component of an integrated library system that will support all library operations. In much the same way that the card catalog is synonymous with the library it represents, the online catalog will be the library of the future. It will of course provide the underlying bibliographic information to support all the library activities, but it will be the library users' "window on the world." Library patrons will be able to use the catalog not only to find out what is in the library, but also to get information from many other sources.

Moving from speculations about the future of the library to the online catalog leads to a few more glimpses of what is in store for us in the years ahead. Foretelling the future is always risky, but here are a few specific predictions about the online catalog itself:

• The terminal keyboard will gradually disappear in favor of touch panels, voice-actuated systems or other forms of direct manipulation.

• Terminals will be smaller, in full color and with better resolution, and diacritics and other special characters sets will be accommodated with ease. Graphic displays will be commonplace so that tables, charts, graphs and other non-textual information can be made available online.

• Computer-to-video disc linkups will combine the indexing capabilities of the computer with the display capabilities of video to make a powerful teaching tool.

• The bibliographic record will be augmented with index information, table of contents, notes, abstracts and other additional information that will make it easier for users to decide if a particular item is of interest.

• The distinction between the library's catalog and the information it represents will blur somewhat. In some cases, users will still search through indexes that will lead them to source materials which may or may not contain the information needed. In other cases, they will be searching for the information directly. Consider, for example, the difference between searching an index of articles from *The New York Times* and searching the text of the articles themselves.

• Online catalogs will be able to accept true natural language requests from users. No longer will "English-like" search statements be required. Instead, users will be able to ask for information as it occurs to them.*

• A "standard online catalog" will gradually emerge so that users can move easily from library to library without having to learn new protocols and procedures every time. The analogy that best describes this is the typical American rental car: anyone who knows how to drive can get in any rental car anywhere in the country and drive it away, confident that its controls and procedures will be standard. This does not necessarily mean that the standard is the best possible alternative (rental cars are rarely high performance vehicles), but it does mean that it is possible for most people to move quickly from one to another without having to learn to drive each time. This same sort of "standardization" is gradually coming to the online catalog and will be taken for granted in the very near future.

CONCLUSION

Many librarians, information scientists, futurists, computer scientists and even library users have stated, in various ways, that "the library is at a crossroads...." The online catalog, the rapid changes in the nature of information—how it is published and distributed—challenge all we have learned about libraries: how they should be organized, the kinds of services they should provide and how patrons should use them. All seem agreed that libraries must somehow adapt to this awesome change in order to survive in the 21st century.

I do not view the situation as bleak, but I do believe that libraries are indeed at a unique place in their history. For centuries, they have been bound by what mankind could do to collect, classify and disseminate information using laborious, time-consuming methods. Now, at last, libraries can escape those limitations if they have the courage and the foresight to do so. For the first time ever, lack of the proper technology is no longer an obstacle. The computer power, data base storage and software are all available to provide the desired services. What remains for libraries to do is to see that they are at the threshold of a new world; to be open to new ideas about how information may be produced, distributed, retrieved and used; to let users tell them what *they* need and then to provide those services as quickly, capably and cheaply as possible.

---

*But I am reminded of an anecdote from the Watergate era. Apparently, a reporter working on the story heard that *The New York Times* was available online and came over to "ask the computer a question." The reporter wanted to know whether the executive power was absolute. Of course, no information retrieval system in existence today (or even in the planning stages) can answer such a question. But in the future, who knows?

Appendix A: Online Catalog Projects—
Four Case Studies

The following case studies illustrate several approaches to, and problems with, public access catalog installations. Included are successful installations at an academic library, a medical library and a corporate library, and one unsuccessful attempt at a large library with more than 1.5 million items in its collection.

SYRACUSE UNIVERSITY LIBRARIES*

The Syracuse University Libraries Information Retrieval System (SULIRS) was developed at the university to provide online bibliographic and circulation control. The system had its beginnings in the late 1960s when the university planned to decentralize technical processing and needed a way to support acquisitions and cataloging. In 1968, Syracuse University Libraries' shelflist was converted to machine-readable form. The resulting file consisted of approximately 470,000 very brief records for materials in the collection.

Background

Early in 1971, a batch-oriented circulation system was created for the libraries by a local computer service organization. At about the same time, the university's Academic Computing Center began to offer some supporting services to the libraries. The first version of an online system, called LIBTEST, was introduced later in 1971 and an in-process system, which included ordering, receiving and accounting, was also installed.

In 1973, the Syracuse University Libraries began to catalog materials through the Online Computer Library Center (OCLC), and in September 1973, a revised circulation system which also ran in batch-mode was developed. At about this time, the name LIBTEST was changed to SULIRS.

---

*Much of the information for this case study was drawn from Gregory N. Bullard, "The Syracuse University Libraries Information Retrieval Systems," *Research Libraries in OCLC: A Quarterly* 7 (July 1982): 1-2.

In 1976, the SULIRS software was redesigned to use OCLC-derived search keys for retrieval, and brief records were replaced by OCLC records. Authority control was added, response time was much improved and an abbreviated record display including author, title, imprint, call number and location was introduced. It was possible to display a full SULIRS record if desired, and to search various numeric fields such as call number, OCLC number and ISBN number.

Also in 1976, additional programs were written to enable OCLC transaction tapes to be loaded directly into the SULIRS data base. In 1978, the circulation system was revised to a quasi-online system using CRT terminals for recording circulation activities; maintaining online exception files for noncirculating items, delinquent borrowers and the like; and updating the master circulation files overnight in a batch operation.

Online Catalog Operation

By 1980, SULIRS was able to display the circulation status along with the bibliographic information. A single CRT terminal was placed in the reference department, and library users were encouraged to experiment with using SULIRS as an online catalog. The response was overwhelmingly positive, even though the system still depended on derived search keys and had no subject search capability. The Syracuse University Libraries closed their nearly 100-year-old card catalogs in favor of the online system in January 1981. Thirty CRT terminals were placed in public areas. The card catalog was frozen; that is, no new cards were added except in the subject catalog, and the rest of the catalog was maintained only to show withdrawals and cross-references. Information about new library materials was available only through SULIRS. The transition was smooth and was welcomed by most library users.

A major new version of SULIRS was installed in May 1981. This version permitted keyword searching on any word in the author, title, series and subject fields as well as allowing these to be combined by using the Boolean AND operator. Additional Boolean combining capabilities were added to permit refining a request in mid-search if the results were too numerous or too ill-defined.

Enhancements to the System

The Syracuse University Libraries continue to make enhancements to SULIRS to assist online catalog users. Major improvements to the circulation system to make it truly an online system and to the acquisitions and accounting modules are also under way. In addition, about 1000 titles per month are being converted to machine-readable form for addition to the SULIRS data base. Campus-wide access through dial-up phone lines has been added. New HELP messages, which are directed to where the user is in a particular search, have been incorporated. These enhancements are consistent with the ultimate objective of the Syracuse University Libraries, which is, according to Gregory N. Bullard, associate director for technical and automated services, "...to put a terminal in every office and wherever students congregate in the university, thus making the catalog widely available."

BETH ISRAEL HOSPITAL LIBRARY*

Background

The PaperChase online catalog was developed by Gary L. Horowitz and Howard L. Bleich, doctors at Beth Israel Hospital, for use by hospital staff members using the hospital library. The system, which is useful for medical searches, provides access to more than 500,000 references from 258 journals covering from 1975 to date. There were several major design assumptions:

- The system should be self-service. There should be no need to read a user's manual, to obtain instruction or to require a trained librarian's assistance to search the library's collections.

- The terminal should be located in the hospital library and should be available at all times.

- The data base should include references for all the materials included in the library. If materials outside the library's holdings are included, they should appear at the end of any search results produced.

- The user should never lose data; that is, if the patron has to interrupt a search session for any reason, the system should keep track of the session and allow the user to resume at the same place at a later time.

- The response time should be very quick because busy clinicians have little time to wait for results.

- The system should be free to the user.

According to Horowitz and Bleich, "The key to computerized literature retrieval is to make the computer interaction self-explanatory." PaperChase requires no sign-in procedure and the program is started by pressing a large, clearly labeled button.

Online Catalog Operation

The system began operating on August 1, 1979, with a single CRT terminal. Neither instructions nor a user's manual were provided. There were no announcements or other publicity about the availability of the system. Under these conditions, on the first day the terminal was available, 12 people used it. The next day 39 people used it to conduct 75 searches; soon it was clear that a second terminal was needed.

During the first year of operation of the PaperChase system, 1032 users conducted 8459 searches and displayed 399,821 references. On the average, each search required 13 minutes of the user's time. For most searches, response was virtually instantaneous.

---

*Much of the information for this case study was drawn from Gary L. Horowitz and Howard L. Bleich, "Paper-Chase: A Computer Program to Search the Medical Literature," *New England Journal of Medicine* 305 (October 1981): 924-930.

Each search consumed an average of 78 seconds of computer processing time at a cost of approximately $2.00 per search. Equipment costs included a CRT terminal (SOROC IQ-120), a Digital Equipment Corp. (DEC) LA-180 printer (together about $3000), a Data General C-350 minicomputer and telecommunications charges for connecting the CRT terminal and the computer. In addition, there is usually the cost of preparing the data base; for the Beth Israel prototype, this was provided free of charge by the National Library of Medicine (NLM).

The PaperChase system has a self-monitoring feature because each search session ends with a brief questionnaire for the user. Of the 8459 searches conducted during the first year of operation, 7708 had completed questionnaires. Users were asked to indicate the purpose of their search and if they found what they were looking for. Results showed that 43.7% of the searches were for patient care, 30.2% for research, 22.2% for teaching and 3.9% for "other." Twelve percent of the users indicated that they did not find what they were looking for and another 14% said they were uncertain. The proportion of successful searches increased for those patrons who had used PaperChase 20 times or more. This suggests that users get better at finding what they want as they gain more experience with the system (or that only those patrons who are successful in getting the desired results continue to use it).

Evaluation and Enhancements

The 8459 searches performed during the first year of operation represented more computerized searches of the general medical literature than at any other medical library in the country. Furthermore, these searches were performed by untrained users who searched the literature themselves whenever they needed to. PaperChase is proving itself to be an excellent, low-cost means of accessing the medical literature and is an attractive option for hospitals, medical schools and other organizations that now must depend on ELHILL or MEDLINE for medical literature searching.

Enhancements to the PaperChase system include plans to add two backfiles from MEDLINE, which will increase the data base to 1.6 million records. Libraries will have the option of searching the full data base or a specific collection. Also, Beth Israel is planning to offer online search services to medical libraries at a price competitive with MEDLARS.

THE DIGITAL EQUIPMENT CORP. LIBRARIES

Background

Digital Equipment Corp. (DEC) has been working on an online union catalog for its corporate libraries. Like many large corporations, DEC has a highly decentralized system of libraries with many locations that are separately managed and funded. In 1980, the librarians formed a group called the Digital Library Network to develop a cooperative system. At about the same time, the corporate headquarters library in Maynard, MA, was experimenting with developing an online catalog. The Digital Library Network became a formal effort in 1981, when it acquired corporate funding, a systems staff, consultants and purchasing authorization. Ten DEC libraries were involved at the outset, and the system now includes 12.

User access from office terminals was the ultimate goal of the online catalog. Because the online catalog would have a large number of infrequent users, a menu-driven approach was selected. In addition, a command language was required to produce the necessary reports from the system.

Other requirements included the need to use OCLC-produced records for the online catalog data base, and to continue cataloging using OCLC for new materials. In addition, there was a need to support local cataloging of DEC proprietary technical reports and other materials which should not be cataloged on the OCLC system.

A DEC internal software review group suggested the Advanced Data Management Data Retrieval System (DRS) as the basis for DEC's online catalog. (Advanced Data Management now markets the BiblioTech automated library system which is derived from the same underlying software.) Advanced Data Management made some alterations to the programs to meet DEC's requirements, but recent enhancements have been made by the DEC systems staff. A standing automation committee of librarians and technical staff meets regularly to discuss the requirements, and to coordinate and evaluate system enhancements.

The catalog runs on a VAX 11/780 minicomputer. Librarians and other users in the various DEC sites access the central computer via ordinary dial-up phone lines and leased lines, and at hard-wired connections in the main library where the computer is located.

Online Catalog Operation

As of mid-1983, in addition to users at office terminals, there were approximately 50 DEC librarians using the system. Six libraries with leased lines have public access terminals. Online assistance features are available so that the online catalog may be used by DEC staff without a librarian's help. A 1983 survey of three DEC libraries over a three-week period showed that the catalog was consulted 2200 times. The subject index was used the most, and the online help messages were used about 20% of the time.

The DEC online catalog data base contains three kinds of records: the cataloging record containing bibliographic data; the item record which contains local site, copy and volume information; and the holdings record which contains site holdings for serials. There are about 40,000 records in the data base. About 15,000 of these are cataloging records and the remainder are primarily the associated item records. DEC maintains a union list of serials in a word processor for its libraries, but it plans to add these records to the online catalog as well.

There are two ways of searching the DEC online catalog—a menu-driven browse mode and a command mode. Call numbers, names, titles, title words and subject words are searchable as well as a local DEC number for DEC publications. The browse mode does not allow the use of Boolean combinations of searches terms.

The command mode can be used to conduct searches using Boolean operators and can also be used to produce various types of reports and items such as new acquisitions lists, selective dissemination of information (SDI) listings and formatted catalogs. The command mode is not "user friendly," but DEC is working on ways to make this part of the system easier to use.

Evaluation and Future Enhancements

DEC has experienced some problems with its online catalog because of the wide variation in the size of the libraries in the network and their geographic dispersion. It is expensive to provide leased lines, and dial-up access is expensive if it requires long-distance phone calls. Some of the larger libraries want COM backup and other safeguards which are not needed by the smaller ones. Eliminating duplicate records from the system and dealing with inadequate subject access points are other problem areas that the DEC library staff has tackled. Among other projects, the DEC staff is working on a thesaurus for an online DEC subject authority file. This file will eliminate any Library of Congress subject headings that are inappropriate for DEC and will add local headings as needed.

AN UNSUCCESSFUL EFFORT

Not all attempts to install online systems have been successful. This case study describes an experiment that failed. To protect the identities of the participants, no actual names are used.

Background

A large library, with a collection of between 1.5 million and 2 million volumes and serving a diverse user group scattered throughout the world, wanted an automated library system including a public access catalog. After long and arduous preparation, a request for proposal (RFP) was issued. Responses were subjected to a lengthy evaluation. The successful bidder was an internationally known software development firm with extensive experience in online applications, but with little first-hand knowledge of library operations. The blueprint for disaster perhaps began right here.

At the time the contract was negotiated, both a very detailed statement of work to be accomplished and a schedule were laid out. The first task to be completed was for the library to prepare a statement of the requirements for the proposed system. The requirements document was to be completed six months after the contract was awarded.

The contractor moved a small staff of people into the library to assist the library staff in framing the requirements document. The first signs of trouble emerged: the library staff was just barely able to describe what its manual systems did, and had a very hazy notion (at best) as to what an online system was supposed to do for the library. Further, two different groups within the library organization assumed responsibility for preparing the document. Neither thought the other knew what it was talking about and both were sure the contractor hadn't the foggiest notion about how libraries worked.

One year later, the requirements document was still not complete. There had been endless drafts during which both sides sought to reach an agreement on what the system should do, so that work could proceed on finishing it. In the meantime, those parts of the system which, it was felt, were not affected by the detailed requirements were started. The vendor—not happy with merely developing an entirely new system—decided that the proper functioning of the new system required development of a new operating system as well. Work began on this underlying software and on some of the applications programs.

The factions within the library still could not agree among themselves or with the vendor on the requirements. Among the areas of disagreement were the form of authority cross-references to be used by online searchers; the number and type of Boolean operators to be supported by the online catalog; and the form of the listings and printed products. Acrimonious memos started flying back and forth, and people from each interest group started taking tape recorders to meetings. As a result of this situation, the contract was renegotiated. Soon afterward, the vendor submitted to the library the Overall Functional Systems Design Specification (OFSDS) in the form of a working paper. At the request of the library, certain minor changes were made in the document, and it was resubmitted for review one month later.

The Review

During the review, the library discussed all sorts of peripheral issues such as personnel assigned to the project, turnover and so forth, but could make few substantive comments about the design. The library began formal review of the OFSDS nearly two months after it was submitted. At the end of this review, the library stated that it had serious reservations about the conceptual basis of the underlying design. Many sections of the document—including the imbedded "Functional Requirements"—were to be rewritten and resubmitted for review. This rewrite was to be a joint effort between the library and the vendor, and was due at the end of the calendar year—nearly 16 months after the start of the project.

At this point, the library informed the vendor that a different phototypesetting device would be used for output, thus changing all the format specifications in the output sections of the detailed systems design. Meanwhile, a clash developed between the vendor's staff and library personnel over such things as normal business hours and proper business attire, which only served to heighten tensions. Two months later, the final revised functional requirements document was completed. Of course, many of the "minor changes" now requested by the library meant "major" programming changes for the vendor.

By spring of the second year, in the belief that the desired system was being developed, the library (which still didn't understand how it would work) asked for a series of "scenarios" describing the processing of various types of materials. Ten such scenarios were prepared for review by the library. After this review, it became clear that the scenarios did or did not meet requirements depending on who was looking at them, and there was no agreement among the library staff even as to which office had the responsibility of deciding.

The project was now entering its third year. The library and the vendor were still wrangling over systems specifications and who had the responsibility for performing certain tasks. The library asked for, and received, samples of certain tools, such as Searcher's

Guides and Report Format Specifiers, that they had asked for. These met with mixed responses.

Finally, still filled with misgivings over whether the system would work, the library asked for a demonstration. By this time, the contract was nearly a year behind schedule and the system had cost a great deal more than had been anticipated. Realizing that if the demonstration were successful the library would have no choice but to continue, the library cancelled the contract at the last possible moment.

Evaluation

It is obvious from the foregoing account that much of the blame for this fiasco rests with the library. However, the vendor, too, made some serious mistakes. These were primarily the result of wrong assumptions—about people, about the library and about technology. The most serious of them were: 1) that anyone can tell you what the system should do; 2) that library systems are just like any other inventory control system; 3) that if the system works technically, it will work organizationally; and finally, 4) that all parties are working toward the same goal.

Appendix B: Patron Access Study
User Questionnaire

PART 1: ABOUT YOUR MOST RECENT SEARCH

INSTRUCTIONS: Please answer these questions about the computer catalog search you just completed.

---

1. I came to this computer search with:
(Mark **ALL** that apply)

a. A complete author's name .... ○
b. Part of an author's name .... ○
c. A complete title .... ○
d. Part of a title .... ○
e. A topic word or words .... ○
f. A subject heading or headings .... ○
g. A complete call number .... ○
h. Part of a call number .... ○

2. By searching this computer catalog I was trying to find:
(Mark **ALL** that apply)

a. A specific book, journal or magazine .... ○
b. Books, journals or magazines on a topic or subject ...... ○
c. Books by a specific author .... ○
d. Information such as publisher, date, spelling of a name, etc. .... ○
e. If a book that I know the library has is available for my use .... ○
f. Another library that has a book, journal or magazine that I want .... ○

3. I searched for what I wanted by:
(Mark **ALL** that apply)

a. A complete author's name .... ○
b. Part of an author's name .... ○
c. A complete title .... ○
d. Part of a title .... ○
e. A topic word or words .... ○
f. A subject heading or headings .... ○
g. A complete call number .... ○
h. Part of a call number .... ○

4. I need this information for:
(Mark **ALL** that apply)

a. Recreational uses .... ○
b. Making or fixing something .... ○
c. My work or job .... ○
d. Personal interest .... ○
e. A hobby .... ○
f. Class or course reading .... ○
g. A course paper or report .... ○
h. A thesis or dissertation .... ○
i. Writing for publication .... ○
j. Teaching or planning a course .... ○
k. Keeping up on a topic or subject .... ○

5. In this computer search I found:
(Mark **ONE** only)

a. More than I was looking for .... ○
b. All that I was looking for .... ○
c. Some of what I was looking for .... ○
d. Nothing I was looking for .... ○

6. In relation to what I was looking for, this computer search was:
(Mark **ONE** only)

a. Very satisfactory .... ○
b. Somewhat satisfactory .... ○
c. Somewhat unsatisfactory .... ○
d. Very unsatisfactory .... ○

7. I came across things of interest other than what I was looking for:

a. YES .... ○
b. NO .... ○

8. I got help in doing this computer catalog search from:
(Mark **ALL** that apply)

a. Printed material or signs .... ○
b. Instructions on the terminal screen .... ○
c. Library staff member .... ○
d. Person nearby .... ○
e. I did not get help .... ○

9. **My overall or general attitude toward the computer catalog is:**
(Mark <u>ONE</u> only)

a. Very favorable .... ○
b. Somewhat favorable .... ○
c. Somewhat unfavorable .... ○
d. Very unfavorable .... ○

10. **Compared to the card, book, or microfiche catalog in this library, the computer catalog is:**
(Mark <u>ONE</u> only)

a. Better .... ○
b. About the same .... ○
c. Worse .... ○
d. Can't decide .... ○

PART 2: YOUR EXPERIENCE WITH COMPUTER CATALOG FEATURES

INSTRUCTIONS: Mark the single column for each question that corresponds most closely to how you feel. If the statement does not apply to your experience at the computer catalog, mark the column, "Does Not Apply".

	STRONGLY AGREE	AGREE	NEITHER AGREE NOR DISAGREE	DISAGREE	STRONGLY DISAGREE	DOES NOT APPLY
11. A computer search by title is difficult	○	○	○	○	○	○
12. A computer search by author is easy	○	○	○	○	○	○
13. A computer search by subject is difficult	○	○	○	○	○	○
14. A computer search by call number is easy	○	○	○	○	○	○
15. A computer search by combined author/title is difficult	○	○	○	○	○	○
16. Remembering commands in the middle of the search is easy	○	○	○	○	○	○
17. Finding the correct subject term is difficult	○	○	○	○	○	○
18. Scanning through a long display (forward or backward) is easy	○	○	○	○	○	○
19. Increasing the result when too little is retrieved is difficult	○	○	○	○	○	○
20. Reducing the result when too much is retrieved is easy	○	○	○	○	○	○
21. Understanding explanations on the screen is difficult	○	○	○	○	○	○
22. Using codes or abbreviations for searching is easy	○	○	○	○	○	○
23. Abbreviations on the screen are easy to understand	○	○	○	○	○	○
24. Locating call numbers on the screen is difficult	○	○	○	○	○	○
25. Searching with a short form of a name or a word (truncation) is easy	○	○	○	○	○	○

	STRONGLY AGREE	AGREE	NEITHER AGREE NOR DISAGREE	DISAGREE	STRONGLY DISAGREE	DOES NOT APPLY
26. Using logical terms like AND, OR, NOT is difficult	○	○	○	○	○	○
27. Remembering the exact sequence or order of commands is easy	○	○	○	○	○	○
28. Understanding the initial instructions on the screen is difficult	○	○	○	○	○	○
29. Understanding the display for a single book, journal or magazine is easy	○	○	○	○	○	○
30. Understanding the display that shows more than a single book, journal or magazine is difficult	○	○	○	○	○	○
31. Interrupting or stopping the display of information is easy	○	○	○	○	○	○
32. Typing in exact spelling, initials, spaces and hyphens is difficult to do	○	○	○	○	○	○
33. Knowing what is included in the computer catalog is easy to remember	○	○	○	○	○	○
34. The order in which items are displayed is easy to understand	○	○	○	○	○	○
35. Displayed messages are too long	○	○	○	○	○	○

	STRONGLY AGREE	AGREE	NEITHER AGREE NOR DISAGREE	DISAGREE	STRONGLY DISAGREE	DOES NOT APPLY
36. Selecting from a list of choices takes too much time	○	○	○	○	○	○
37. Entering commands when I want to during the search process is difficult	○	○	○	○	○	○
38. The rate at which the computer responds is too slow	○	○	○	○	○	○
39. The availability of signs and brochures is adequate	○	○	○	○	○	○
40. Signs and brochures are not very useful	○	○	○	○	○	○
41. The staff advice is often not helpful	○	○	○	○	○	○
42. It is hard to find a free terminal	○	○	○	○	○	○

YOU ARE MORE THAN HALF - WAY DONE

PART 3: IMPROVING THE COMPUTER CATALOG

INSTRUCTIONS: Select the response or responses that best reflect your views about changes that should be made in the computer catalog.

43. When I use the computer catalog terminal: (Mark YES or NO)

	YES	NO
a. The keyboard is confusing to use	○	○
b. There is too much glare on the screen	○	○
c. The letters and numbers are easy to read	○	○
d. The lighting around the terminal is too bright	○	○
e. There is enough writing space at the terminal	○	○
f. Nearby noise is distracting	○	○
g. The terminal table is too high or too low	○	○
h. The printer is easy to use	○	○

44. Select up to FOUR additional features you would like this computer catalog to have:

a. Providing step by step instructions ○
b. Searching by any word or words in a title ○
c. Searching by any word or words in a subject heading ○
d. Limiting search results by date of publication ○
e. Limiting search results by language ○
f. Ability to search by journal title abbreviations ○
g. Ability to change the order in which items are displayed ○
h. Ability to view a list of words related to my search words ○
i. Ability to search for illustrations and bibliographies ○
j. Ability to search by call number ○
k. Ability to print search results ○
l. Ability to search a book's table of contents, summary or index ○
m. Ability to know if a book is checked out ○
n. Ability to tell where a book is located in the library ○
o. None ○

45. Select up to FOUR computer catalog service improvements you would like the library to make:

a. More terminals ○
b. Terminals at locations other than near the card catalog ○
c. Terminals at places other than library buildings ○
d. A chart of commands posted at the terminal ○
e. A manual or brochure at the terminal ○
f. An instruction manual for purchase ○
g. Training sessions ○
h. Slide/tape/cassette training program ○
i. None ○

46. Select up to FOUR kinds of material you would like to see added to the computer catalog:

a. Dissertations ○
b. Motion picture films ○
c. Government publications ○
d. Journal or magazine titles ○
e. Maps ○
f. Manuscripts ○
g. Music scores ○
h. Newspapers ○
i. Phonograph records or tapes ○
j. Technical reports ○
k. More of the library's older books ○
l. None ○
m. Other ○

47. BRIEFLY DESCRIBE ANY OTHER PROBLEMS WITH THIS COMPUTER CATALOG OR CHANGES YOU WOULD LIKE MADE TO IT: ○

PART 4: ABOUT YOURSELF

INSTRUCTIONS: Your responses are confidential. Please do not write your name anywhere on this questionnaire.

48. I come to this library:

a. Daily .... ○
b. Weekly .... ○
c. Monthly .... ○
d. About four times a year .... ○
e. About once a year .... ○
f. Not before today .... ○

49. I use this computer catalog:

a. Every library visit .... ○
b. Almost every visit .... ○
c. Occasionally .... ○
d. Rarely .... ○
e. Not before today .... ○

50. I use this library's book, card or microfilm catalog:

a. Every visit .... ○
b. Almost every visit .... ○
c. Occasionally .... ○
d. Rarely .... ○
e. Never .... ○

51. I use a computer system other than the library's computer catalog:

a. Daily .... ○
b. Weekly .... ○
c. Monthly .... ○
d. About four times a year .... ○
e. About once a year .... ○
f. Never .... ○

52. I first heard about this computer catalog from: (Mark ONE only)

a. Noticing a terminal in the library .... ○
b. Library tour, orientation or demonstration ...... ○
c. An article or written announcement .... ○
d. A course instructor .... ○
e. A friend or family member .... ○
f. Library staff .... ○

53. I learned how to use this computer catalog: (Mark ALL that apply)

a. From a friend or someone at a nearby terminal .... ○
b. Using printed instructions .... ○
c. Using instructions on the terminal screen .... ○
d. From the library staff .... ○
e. From a library course or orientation .... ○
f. From a slide/tape/cassette program .... ○
g. By myself without any help .... ○

54. My age group is:

a. 14 and under .... ○
b. 15 - 19 years .... ○
c. 20 - 24 years .... ○
d. 25 - 34 years .... ○
e. 35 - 44 years .... ○
f. 45 - 54 years .... ○
g. 55 - 64 years .... ○
h. 65 and over .... ○

55. I am:

a. Female .... ○
b. Male .... ○

56. Mark your current or highest educational level: (Mark ONE only)

a. Grade School or Elementary School .... ○
b. High School or Secondary School .... ○
c. Some College or University .... ○
d. College or University Graduate .... ○

If you **are not** completing this questionnaire at a college or university, please stop here. Thank you.

If you **are** completing this questionnaire at a college or university, please continue.

57. The category that best describes my academic area is: (Mark ONE only)

a. Arts and Humanities .... ○
b. Physical/Biological Sciences .... ○
c. Social Sciences .... ○
d. Business/Management .... ○
e. Education .... ○
f. Engineering .... ○
g. Medical/Health Sciences .... ○
h. Law .... ○
i. Major not declared .... ○
j. Interdisciplinary .... ○

58. The main focus of my academic work at the present time is:
(Mark **ALL** that apply)

a. Course Work .... O
b. Teaching .... O
c. Research .... O

59. My present affiliation with this college or university is:

a. Freshman/Sophomore .... O
b. Junior/Senior .... O
c. Graduate - masters level .... O
d. Graduate - doctoral level .... O
e. Graduate - professional school .... O
f. Faculty .... O
g. Staff .... O
h. Other .... O

Thank you for participating in this study of the computer catalog. This completes the questionnaire. Please return it.

SUPPLEMENTARY QUESTIONNAIRE ITEMS

60. O O O O O O O O O O O O O
61. O O O O O O O O O O O O O
62. O O O O O O O O O O O O O
63. O O O O O O O O O O O O O
64. O O O O O O O O O O O O O

Appendix C: Patron Access Study Non-user Questionnaire

1. I have not used the computer catalog up to now because:
   (Mark ALL that apply)

   a. I do not like to use computers .... O
   b. I did not know there was a computer catalog .... O

   c. I do not know where it is .... O
   d. I have not had time to learn to use it .... O

   e. I have not taken training sessions on how to use it .... O
   f. There has not been any staff at the terminals to assist me in using it .... O

   g. The terminals were all in use when I wanted to use it .... O

   h. I have not needed to use any library catalog recently .... O
   i. The card catalog is easier to use .... O
   j. The card catalog contains more of the information I need .... O
   k. I am a visitor or infrequent user of this library .... O

2. How much time do you think it takes to learn to use the computer catalog?

   a. A day or more .... O
   b. Between 1/2 of a day and a day .... O
   c. Between an hour and 1/2 of a day .... O
   d. Between 30 minutes and an hour .... O
   e. Between 15 minutes and 30 minutes .... O
   f. 15 minutes or less .... O

3. How difficult or easy do you think it would be to learn to use the computer catalog?

   a. Very difficult .... O
   b. Somewhat difficult .... O
   c. Somewhat easy .... O
   d. Very easy .... O

4. My overall or general attitude toward the computer catalog is:

   a. Very favorable .... O
   b. Somewhat favorable .... O
   c. Somewhat unfavorable .... O
   d. Very unfavorable .... O

5. How likely are you to use the computer catalog in the future?

   a. Very likely .... O
   b. Somewhat likely .... O
   c. Somewhat unlikely .... O
   d. Very unlikely .... O

6. Compared to the card, book, or microfiche catalog in this library the computer catalog is:
   (Mark ONE only)

   a. Better .... O
   b. About the same .... O
   c. Worse .... O
   d. Can't decide .... O

7. I come to this library:

   a. Daily .... O
   b. Weekly .... O
   c. Monthly .... O
   d. About four times a year .... O
   e. About once a year .... O
   f. Not before today .... O

8. I use this library's book, card or microfilm catalog:

   a. Every visit .... O
   b. Almost every visit .... O
   c. Occasionally .... O
   d. Rarely .... O
   e. Not before today .... O

9. I use a computer system other than the library's computer catalog:

a. Daily .... ⚪
b. Weekly .... ⚪
c. Monthly .... ⚪
d. About four times a year .... ⚪
e. About once a year .... ⚪
f. Never .... ⚪

10. My age group is:

a. 14 and under .... ⚪
b. 15 - 19 years .... ⚪
c. 20 - 24 years .... ⚪
d. 25 - 34 years .... ⚪
e. 35 - 44 years .... ⚪
f. 45 - 54 years .... ⚪
g. 55 - 64 years .... ⚪
h. 65 and over .... ⚪

11. I am:

a. Female .... ⚪
b. Male .... ⚪

12. Mark your current or highest educational level: (Mark ONE only)

a. Grade School or Elementary School .... ⚪
b. High School or Secondary School .... ⚪
c. Some College or University .... ⚪
d. College or University Graduate .... ⚪

If you are not completing this questionnaire at a college or university, please stop here. Thank you.

If you are completing this questionnaire at a college or university, please continue.

13. The category that best describes my academic area is: (Mark ONE only)

a. Arts and Humanities .... ⚪
b. Physical/Biological Sciences .... ⚪
c. Social Sciences .... ⚪
d. Business/Management .... ⚪
e. Education .... ⚪
f. Engineering .... ⚪
g. Medical/Health Sciences .... ⚪
h. Law .... ⚪
i. Major not declared .... ⚪
j. Interdisciplinary .... ⚪

14. The main focus of my academic work at the present time is: (Mark ALL that apply)

a. Course Work .... ⚪
b. Teaching .... ⚪
c. Research .... ⚪

15. My present affiliation with this college or university is:

a. Freshman/Sophomore .... ⚪
b. Junior/Senior .... ⚪
c. Graduate - masters level .... ⚪
d. Graduate - doctoral level .... ⚪
e. Graduate - professional school .... ⚪
f. Faculty .... ⚪
g. Staff .... ⚪
h. Other .... ⚪

Thank you for participating in this study of the computer catalog. This completes the questionnaire. Please return it.

SUPPLEMENTARY QUESTIONNAIRE ITEMS

16. ⚪⚪⚪⚪⚪⚪⚪⚪⚪⚪⚪⚪⚪
17. ⚪⚪⚪⚪⚪⚪⚪⚪⚪⚪⚪⚪⚪
18. ⚪⚪⚪⚪⚪⚪⚪⚪⚪⚪⚪⚪⚪
19. ⚪⚪⚪⚪⚪⚪⚪⚪⚪⚪⚪⚪⚪

Appendix D: Selected Online Public Access Catalog Installations

Beth Israel Hospital
330 Brookline Ave.
Boston, MA 02215
(617) 735-2253
Contact: Dr. Howard L. Bleich
System: PaperChase
Hardware: Data General C-350
    minicomputer
Size: 500,000+ records, 4 terminals

Claremont Colleges Libraries
800 Dartmouth St.
Claremont, CA 91711
(714) 621-8045
Contact: Adrienne Long
System: Total Library System (TLS)
Hardware: Hewlett-Packard 3000 Series II
    minicomputer
Size: 70,000+ records, 8 terminals

Cleveland Public Library
325 Superior Ave.
Cleveland, OH 44114
(216) 623-2800
Contact: Dr. Ervin Gaines
System: Data Research Associates, ATLAS
Hardware: 2 DEC VAX 11/780 mini-
    computers
Size: 1 million+ records, 85+ terminals

Dallas Public Library
1954 Commerce St.
Dallas, TX 75201
(214) 749-4321
Contact: Antoinette L. Johnson
System: LSCAN
Hardware: ITEL AS5/1 mainframe
Size: 450,000+ records, 200 terminals

Dartmouth College
Dartmouth College Libraries
Hanover, NH 03755
(603) 646-2574
Contact: Emily G. Fayen
System: Dartmouth Online Catalog
Hardware: DEC VAX 11/750 mini-
    computer
Size: 400,000+ records, 300+ terminals
System marketed by: Bibliographic
    Retrieval Services (BRS), 1200 Route
    7, Latham, NY 12010

Digital Equipment Corp. (DEC)
77 Reed Rd.
Hudson, MA 01749
(617) 568-4000
Contact: Joyce A. Ward
System: BiblioTech
Hardware: DEC VAX 11/780 minicom-
    puter
Size: 40,000+ records, 50 terminals

Evanston Public Library
1703 Orrington Ave.
Evanston, IL 60201
(312) 866-0300
Contact: Trarie Kottkamp
System: CL Systems, Inc.
Hardware: DEC PDP 11/34
   minicomputer
Size: 200,000+ records, 15 terminals

Jefferson County Public Library
10200 West 20 Ave.
Lakewood, CO 80215
(303) 238-8411
Contact: Billie Bleisner
System: Jeffcat
Hardware: Harris 1670, Univac 1100/161
   minicomputers
Size: 450,000+ records, 25 terminals

Library of Congress
Washington, DC 20540
(202) 287-5000
Contact: Linda Arret
System: MUMS/SCORPIO
Hardware: IBM 3033, Amdahl 470/V6
   mainframes
Size: 1.8 million records, 3000 terminals

Mankato State University
Memorial Library
Haywood and Ellis St.
Mankato, MN 56001
Contact: Dale Carrison
System: Minnesota State University
   System's Project for Automation of
   Library Systems (MSUS/PALS)
Hardware: Univac 1100 Model 80A
Size: 600,000+ records, 120 terminals

Mountain View Elementary School
Broomfield, CO 80020
(303) 466-1791
Contact: Betty Costa
System: Computer Cat
Hardware: Apple II Plus
Size: 4000+ records, 1 terminal

National Library of Medicine (NLM)
8600 Rockville Pike
Bethesda, MD 20209
(301) 496-1936
Contact: Frieda Weise
System: Integrated Library System (ILS)
Hardware: DEC, Data General, IBM mini-
   computers
Size: varies, depending on the hardware
   configuration
Locations: Carnegie Mellon University,
   New Hampshire State Library, Oak
   Ridge National Laboratory, NLM
System: CITE
Hardware: IBM 3033 mainframe
Size: 450,000+ records, 6 terminals

Northwestern University Library
Northwestern University
1935 Sheridan Rd.
Evanston, IL 60201
(312) 492-7640
Contact: Brian Nielsen
System: Library User Information Service
   (LUIS)
Hardware: IBM 4331-1 mainframe
Size: 500,000+ records, 25 terminals

Ohio State University
1858 Neil Ave. Mall
Columbus, OH 43210
(614) 422-9481
Contact: Marsha McClintock
System: Library Control System (LCS)
Hardware: Amdahl V7 mainframe
Size: 1.7+ million records, 200 terminals

Online Computer Library Center, Inc.
   (OCLC)
6565 Frantz Rd.
Dublin, OH 43017
(614) 764-6000
Contact: Charles Hildreth
System: OCLC
Hardware: 10 Sigma 9 mainframes
Size: 7.5+ million records

Pikes Peak Regional Library District
Penrose Public Library
20 North Cascade
Colorado Springs, CO 80901
(303) 473-2080
Contact: Kenneth Dowlin
System: Maggies Place
Hardware: DEC PDP 11/70
Size: 400,000+ records, 100 terminals

Pomona Public Library
625 South Garey Ave.
PO Box 2271
Pomona, CA 91769
(714) 620-2043
System: CTI Library Systems, Inc.
Hardware: Prime 550 II
Size: 165,000 records, 30+ terminals

Research Libraries Group (RLG)
Jordan Quadrangle
Stanford, CA 94305
(415) 328-0920
Contact: Barbara Brown
System: Research Libraries Information
   Network (RLIN)
Hardware: IBM 3081 mainframe
Size: 3.2 million records, 300+ terminals

Southeastern Library Information
   Network (SOLINET)
Plaza Level
400 Colony Square
1201 Peachtree St., NE
Atlanta, GA 30361
(404) 892-0943
Contact: Randall Cravy
System: Washington Library Network
   (WLN)
Hardware: Burroughs B7800 mainframe
Size: 300,000+ records, 30 terminals

Stephen F. Austin State University
Ralph W. Steen Library
Nacogdoches, TX 75962
(713) 569-4217
Contact: Al Cage
System: DataPhase
Hardware: Data General Eclipse S/130
   minicomputer
Size: 100,000+ records, 20 terminals

Syracuse University
Syracuse University Libraries
222 Waverly Ave.
Syracuse, NY 13210
(315) 423-2093
Contact: Gregory Bullard
System: Syracuse University Libraries
   Information Retrieval System
   (SULIRS)
Hardware: IBM 4341 mainframe
Size: 500,000+ records, 50+ terminals

University of California
Division of Library Automation
186 University Hall
Berkeley, CA 94720
(415) 642-9485
Contact: Edwin Brownrigg
System: MELVYL
Hardware: Magnuson M 80/4 mainframe
Size: 700,000+ records, 100+ terminals

University of Guelph
Guelph, Ontario
Canada N1G 2W1
(519) 824-4120
Contact: Margaret Beckman
System: Geac
Hardware: Geac 6000 minicomputer
Size: 600,000+ records, 30+ terminals

University of New Brunswick
Harriet Irving Library
Fredericton, New Brunswick
Canada E3B 5H5
(506) 453-4740
Contact: Brian Lesser
System: Phoenix
Hardware: IBM 3030 mainframe
Size: 180,000+ records, 30 terminals

University of Toronto Library
130 St. George St.
Toronto, Ontario
Canada M5S 1A5
(416) 978-7171
Contact: Sonia Hackett
System: Library Collection Management
    System (LCMS), University of
    Toronto Library Automation System
    (UTLAS)
Hardware: Data General Eclipse S/200
    minicomputer
Size: 100,000+ records, 30 terminals

Virginia Tech Library
113 Burruss Hall
Blacksburg, VA 24061
(703) 961-5847
Contact: Carl Lee
System: Virginia Tech Library System
    (VTLS)
Hardware: Hewlett Packard HP 3000
    Series III minicomputer
Size: 500,000+ records, 10 terminals

Washington University School of Medicine
4580 Scott Ave.
St. Louis, MO 63110
(314) 889-5400
Contact: Betsy Kelly
System: Bibliographic Access and Control
    System (BACS)
Hardware: DEC PDP 11/44 minicomputer
Size: 25,000+ records, 10 terminals

West Valley Community College District
14000 Fruitvale
Saratoga, CA 95070
(408) 867-2200
Contact: Mary Hoeber
System: Universal Library Systems
    (ULISYS). System shared by Mission
    College and West Valley College
Hardware: DEC PDP 11/70 minicomputer
Size: 80,000+ records, 30+ terminals

WLN Library Services
Washington Library Network
AJ-11
Olympia, WA 98504
(206) 459-6518
Contact: Bruce Zigman
System: WLN
Hardware: Amdahl mainframe
Size: 2.7 million records, 106 libraries

Appendix E: Online Catalog System Vendors*

Advanced Data Management
c/o Comstow Information Services
302 Boxboro Rd.
Stow, MA 01775

Avatar Systems, Inc.
11325 Seven Locks Rd.
Suite 205
Potomac, MD 20854

Beth Israel Hospital
330 Brookline Ave.
Boston, MA 02215

Bibliographic Retrieval Services, Inc.
    (BRS)
1200 Rte. 7
Latham, NY 12110

Biblio-Techniques
8511 Lake Lucinda Dr., SW
Olympia, WA 98502

Carlyle Systems, Inc.
600 Bancroft Way
Berkeley, CA 94710

CL Systems, Inc. (CLSI)
81 Norwood Ave.
Newtonville, MA 02160

Claremont Colleges Library
800 Dartmouth St.
Claremont, CA 91711

Colorado Computer Systems, Inc.
3005 W. 74th Ave.
Westminster, CO 80030

CTI Library Systems, Inc.
120 E. 300 North
Provo, UT 84061

Dallas Public Library
1954 Commerce St.
Dallas, TX 75201

DataPhase Systems, Inc.
3770 Broadway
Kansas City, MO 64111

Data Research Associates
9270 Olive Blvd.
St. Louis, MO 63132

DTI Data Trek, Inc.
121 West E St.
Encinitas, CA 92024

Easy Data Systems Ltd.
401-1200 Lonsdale Ave.
North Vancouver, British Columbia
Canada V7M 3H6

*Some institutions that appeared in Appendix D are repeated here, since they are both locations of installed catalogs and catalog vendors.

Geac Canada Ltd.
305 Steelcase Rd. West
Markham, Ontario
Canada L3R 1B3

IBM Corp.
10401 Fernwood Rd.
Bethesda, MD 20034

Jefferson County Public Library
10200 West 20th Ave.
Lakewood, CA 80215

Library of Congress
Washington, DC 20540

Mankato State University
Minnesota State University System
Mankato, MN 56001

National Technical Information Service
   (NTIS)
5275 Port Royal Rd.
Springfield, VA 22161

Northwestern University
1935 Sheridan Rd.
Evanston, IL 60201

Ohio State University
1858 Neil Ave. Mall
Columbus, OH 43210

Online Computer Library Center
6565 Frantz Rd.
Dublin, OH 43017

Online Computer Systems, Inc.
20010 Century Blvd.
Suite 101
Germantown, MD 20874

Pikes Peak Regional Library District
PO Box 1579
Colorado Springs, CO 80901

Research Libraries Group
Jordan Quadrangle
Stanford, CA 94305

Southeastern Library Network
   (SOLINET)
Plaza Level
400 Colony Square
Atlanta, GA 30361

Syracuse University
222 Waverly Ave.
Syracuse, NY 13210

Universal Library Systems
1571 Bellevue Ave.
West Vancouver, British Columbia
Canada V7 V 1A5

University of California
Division of Library Automation
186 University Hall
Berkeley, CA 94720

University of New Brunswick
Harriet Irving Library
Fredericton, New Brunswick
Canada E3B 5H5

University of Toronto Library
   Automation Systems (UTLAS, Inc.)
80 Bloor St. West, 2nd Floor
Toronto, Ontario
Canada M5S 2V1

Virginia Tech Library Automation Project
113 Burruss Hall
Blacksburg, VA 24061

Washington Library Network
Washington State Library
AJ-11
Olympia, WA 98504

Washington University School of Medicine
4580 Scott Ave.
St. Louis, MO 63110

Glossary

Anglo-American Cataloging Rules: A set of rules and guidelines used for cataloging materials. The second edition (AACR2) was published in 1978.

ANSI: American National Standards Institute. An organization that acts as a national clearinghouse and coordinator for voluntary standards in the United States, for programming languages, computer equipment, telecommunications protocols, etc.

Applications software: The computer programs written to perform various functions such as online searching, listing citations, checking out books and so forth.

ASCII: American Standard Code for Information Interchange. This is one of a number of standard methods for representing data to be processed by a computer.

Authority file: A data file containing the established or chosen headings to be used for names, subjects or series. These headings are now established according to the second edition of the *Anglo-American Cataloging Rules* (AACR2).

BASIC: Beginners All Purpose Symbolic Instruction Code. A programming language with simple syntax and few commands often used on minicomputers and microcomputers.

Baud rate: A measure of the rate of data flow between two pieces of equipment such as a computer and a terminal or a terminal and an attached printer. Typical baud rates range from 300 bits per second (or about 30 characters per second) to 9600 bits per second.

Bit: The smallest unit of information a computer can recognize. Bits can have one of two values, "on" or "off," represented by one or zero. All information handled by a computer is represented by various combinations of these two values.

Byte: A collection of bits (usually eight, but sometimes nine) that are taken together to represent a character (e.g., a letter of the alphabet, a digit or some other symbol). The term byte is often used to indicate the amount of room needed to store the data, such as 1000 bytes, 1 million bytes, etc.

COBOL: COmmon Business-Oriented Language. A high-level language widely used in business applications software.

CPU: Central Processing Unit. The part of a computer that actually performs the manipulations of the data. The terms CPU and computer are sometimes used interchangeably. Properly, however, "CPU" refers to the central processing portion of the computer and not to tape drives, disk drives, printers and other auxiliary equipment.

CRT: Cathode Ray Tube. A terminal with a video display screen. This is sometimes called a VDT, or video display terminal.

Data base: The entire collection of machine-readable data or records stored in a computer.

Data base management system: Also referred to as the DBMS or data base manager, this is a set of computer programs that enables the system to retrieve and report information according to various logical criteria. In a library system, the data base manager might make it possible to retrieve information on all books purchased after June 1983, for example.

Distributed processing: An arrangement whereby various parts of a large operation are handled by different computers in different locations. In a library, for example, overdue notices might be generated and printed out by a microcomputer at the circulation desk while monthly acquisitions statistics are produced by another computer.

Field: Part of a record. The specific area used for a particular category of data such as author name, subject heading, call number, etc.

Firmware: A term used to describe a type of software that has been implemented as a piece of hardware; i.e., software that has been encoded on a chip or circuit board. A piece of firmware usually performs one function.

Fixed-length field: A field that is of predetermined and constant length, rather than being varied according to the actual extent of the contents.

Fixed-length record: A machine-readable record of predetermined and constant length. For example, a patron record for an online circulation system might allow 25 characters for the name, 25 for the address, 12 for the phone number, 2 for the patron class and 50 for any comments. Thus, the record would have a fixed length of 114 characters.

Floppy disk: An inexpensive medium for storing data, frequently used in microcomputers. Floppy disks look like 45 rpm records that are permanently sealed in a paper jacket with a small window. They generally come in 8-inch and 5¼-inch sizes.

FORTRAN: FORmula TRANslation. A high-level programming language often used for scientific applications.

Hard Disk: A data storage medium. Hard disks generally are more durable, hold more data, and cost more than floppy disks. They also provide faster access to the data. Libraries almost always need hard disk drives for online catalog applications because of the large amounts of data involved.

Hardware: The computer system, usually including the central processing unit, the tape drives, disk drives, printers and other parts of the system that come in metal (or plastic) cases.

Index: A means of identifying individual records or sets of records in a data base according to the value or values of various data elements or fields, such as author, title, call number, etc. In general, any data element contained in a record may be used to create an index for that record.

Inverted file: A file created from another by altering the sequence of the fields or by creating a cross index to another file so that a key word identifies a record. This technique is often used to minimize access time and to economize on storage requirements.

Machine-readable: Information that has been encoded in a form that allows it to be processed by a computer.

Magnetic tape: A low cost, high volume data storage medium frequently used to transfer data from one location to another or from one part of a system to another. Magnetic tapes usually have seven or nine tracks on which data are stored. The tapes may be reel-to-reel, cassettes or cartridges.

Mainframe: A full-sized computer (usually costing more than $1 million) that is based on a CPU, the memory of which is normally measured in millions of bytes (megabytes).

MARC: MAchine Readable Cataloging. MARC is the standard format for representing library cataloging information that is to be stored, used or transmitted in machine-readable form. MARC is an international standard.

Memory: The part of the CPU that holds the information being processed.

Microcomputer: A microprocessor with associated input and output capability. Generally distinguishable from a minicomputer by lower price, processing speed and capacity.

Microprocessor: A complete computer processor on a single integrated-circuit chip approximately the size of a dime. These chips have all the processing power of the early room-sized computers.

Minicomputer: A physically compact digital device that has a CPU, at least one input-output device and a primary storage capacity of at least 4000 characters.

MIS: Management Information System. A data base management system that is used to provide management information.

Modem: A contraction of modulator-demodulator. It is used to make signals from a computer or terminals compatible with communications facilities (such as telephone lines).

OCR: Optical Character Recognition. A technique of scanning printed text electronically and converting the images—both letters and digits—into encoded form for the computer.

Operating system: A super program, or organized set of computer software, that controls the overall operations of a computer. This software is needed in addition to the applications software that is tailored to perform specific tasks.

Peripherals: The other hardware components of a computer system besides the CPU. Peripherals include devices such as tape drives, disk drives, line printers, consoles, terminals and so on.

Real time: A computer operating mode under which data are received, processed and returned so quickly as to seem instantaneous. In a man-machine sense, real time implies an interactive operation.

Record: A unit of information consisting of a group of data elements or fields which may logically be grouped together and considered as one. For example, an entire bibliographic citation may be considered as one record, containing author, title, imprint, collation, call number and other information. Similarly, all of the information needed about a library user for an online circulation system might be stored as a patron record.

Record length: The amount of space (usually measured in characters or bytes) needed to store the record in machine-readable form. The record length may be fixed or variable.

Software: Any programs that tell the computer how to manipulate data.

Storage: In contrast to memory, usually used to indicate where the data are kept outside of the CPU. Sometimes called remote storage.

System software: Computer programs that control the internal workings of the computer. The operating system and the data base manager (if there is one) are both considered part of the system software.

Terminal: A device through which users communicate with the computer system. In a library, a terminal may be used for circulation, online access or any number of other functions. A terminal usually has a keyboard and some sort of display capability such as a printer and/or CRT.

Time sharing: A method of sharing the resources of one computer system among several users so that it appears to each user as though the system is dedicated to that individual's particular application. Online catalog and circulation systems usually work this way. Each user has a terminal and can perform various functions as though the computer were dedicated to his or her use.

Turnkey system: An entire computer system, including hardware, software, applications programs, training programs, installation and other special features, prepared by a vendor and sold to a customer as a package. Many automated library systems are offered as turn-key systems. The term turnkey means that the system will do everything it is supposed to do as soon as it is turned over to the customer.

Update: The process of keeping machine-readable files current. Update may include adding new records, data elements or fields; deleting records, data elements or fields; or changing existing data elements or fields.

Variable-length record: A record whose length may vary from instance to instance. For example, a bibliographic citation might be very long or very short depending on the amount of cataloging information needed to describe the item.

Selected Bibliography

"Artificial Intelligence: The Second Computer Age Begins." *Business Week*, March 8, 1982, pp. 66-75.

Beckman, Margaret M. "Online Catalogs and Library Users." *Library Journal* (November 1, 1982): 2043-2047.

Boss, Richard W. *The Library Manager's Guide to Automation, 2nd Edition*. White Plains, NY: Knowledge Industry Publications, Inc., in press.

Brownrigg, Edwin B., and Lynch, Clifford A. "Online Catalogs: Through a Glass Darkly." *Information Technology and Libraries* (March 1983): 104-115.

Carter, Ruth C. and Bruntjen, Scott. *Data Conversion*. White Plains, NY: Knowledge Industry Publications, Inc., 1983.

Cochrane, Pauline A. "'Friendly' Catalog Forgives User Errors." *American Libraries* (May 1982): 303-306.

— — —. "Subject Access in the Online Catalog." *Research Libraries in OCLC* 5 (January 1982).

Connor, Ursula. "Success of Office Automation Depends on User Acceptance, not High Technology." *Computerworld: Special Report*, September 14, 1981, pp. 46-49.

Council on Library Resources, Inc. "On-line Public Access to Library Bibliographic Data Bases: Developments, Issues, and Priorities." OCLC, Inc. and the Research Libraries Group, Inc., Dartmouth College, Hanover, NH, September 1980.

Division of Library Automation and Library Research and Analysis Group, University of California at Berkeley. *Users Look at Online Catalogs: Results of a National Survey of Users and Non-users of Online Catalogs*. Final report to the Council on Library Resources, November 16, 1982.

Elam, Philip G. "Human Considerations." *Computerworld: In Depth*, March 31, 1980.

Epstein, Susan Baerg. "Buy, Build, Adapt—or Forget It!" *Library Journal* (May 1, 1983): 888-889.

— — —. "Converting Bibliographic Records for Automation: Some Options." *Library Journal* (March 1, 1983): 474-476

Faibisoff, Sylvia G. "Is There a Future for the End User In Online Bibliographic Searching?" *Special Libraries* (October, 1981): 347-353.

Fasana, Paul. "1981 and Beyond: Visions and Decisions." *Journal of Library Automation* 13 (2) (June 1980): 96-107.

Frazier, Patrick. "Alien in the Reading Room." *American Libraries* (October 1980): 536-539.

Goldfinger, Edward. "A Manager's Guide to Computer Software." *Inc.*, June 1980, p. 79-89.

— — —. "A Manager's Guide to Computer Systems." *Inc.*, May 1980, p. 101-107.

Goldstein, Charles M. and Ford, William H. "The User-Cordial Interface." *Online Review* 2 (3) (1978): 269-275.

Hegarty, Kevin. *More Joy of Contracts: An Epicurean Approach to Negotiation.* Tacoma, WA: Tacoma Public Library, 1981.

Hildreth, Charles R. *Online Public Access Catalogs: The User Interface.* Dublin, OH: OCLC Library Information, and Computer Science Series, 1982.

Hodges, Parker. "An Executive's Guide to Acronyms." *Output* (September 1980): 42-46.

— — —. "Fear of Automation." *Output* (August 1980): 34-40.

Horny, Karen L. "Online Catalogs: Coping with the Choices." *The Journal of Academic Librarianship* 8 (1) (March 1982): 14-19.

Kemeny, John G. "A Library for 2000 A.D." *M.I.T. Centennial Lecture Series.* Cambridge, MA: Massachusetts Institute of Technology, March 27, 1961.

Lacey, Paul A. "Views of a Luddite." *College and Research Libraries* (March 1982): 111-123.

Lanson, Gerald. "Information Please." *Science 82* (March 1982): 38-41.

Laver, Tina. "Online Public Access Catalogs: The Future in the Present." *Humanities Report* (April 1982): 11-15.

Lindsay, E.J. "Familiarity, Use, and Importance of Information on Library Catalog Cards." Technical Report No. 9. Hanover, NH: Dartmouth College, September 25, 1978.

Lister Hill National Center for Biomedical Communications, National Library of Medicine. "The Integrated Library System: Overview and Status." Bethesda, MD: Lister Hill National Center, October 1979.

Lundeen, Gerald. "Microcomputers in Personal Information Systems." *Special Libraries* (April 1981): 127-137.

Malinconico, S. Michael. "Listening to the Resistance." *Library Journal* (February 15, 1983): 353-355.

— — —. "Mass Storage Technology and File Organization." *Journal of Library Automation* 13 (2) (June 1980): 77-87.

Marcum, Deanna and Boss, Richard. "Information Technology." *Wilson Library Bulletin* (January 1981): 396-398.

Matthews, Joseph R. *Comparative Information for Automated Circulation Systems.* Grass Valley, CA: 1981.

— — —. *Public Access to Online Catalogs: A Planning Guide for Managers.* Weston, CT: Online, Inc., 1982.

— — —. "20 Qs and As on Automated Integrated Library Systems." *American Libraries* (June 1982): 366-371.

— — —. "The Automated Library System Marketplace, 1982: Change and More Change." *Library Journal* (March 15, 1983): 547-553.

Moynihan, John A. "What Users Want." *Datamation* (April 1982): 116-118.

Nelson, Ted. "A New Home for the Mind." *Datamation* (March 1982): 167-180.

Petroski, Henry. "The Electronic Newspaper: An Easy Route to 1984?" *The Futurist* (August 1982): 59-60.

Raben, Joseph. "Advent of the Post-Gutenberg University." *Acadcme* (March-April 1983): 21-27.

Rossman, Parker. "The Coming Great Electronic Encyclopedia." *The Futurist* (August 1982): 53-57.

Salmon, Stephen R. "Characteristics of Online Catalogs." *Library Resources and Technical Services* 27 (1) (January/March 1983): 36-67.

Schneiderman, Ben. "How to Design with the User in Mind." *Datamation* (April 1982): 125-126.

Seiler, Lauren H. and Raben, Joseph. "The Electronic Journal." *Society* (September/October 1981): 76-83.

Sharer, Laura. "Pinpointing Requirements." *Datamation* (April 1981): 139-151.

Sharp, John R. *Some Fundamentals of Information Retrieval.* New York: London House and Maxwell, 1965.

Simpson, Henry. "A Human-Factors Style Guide for Program Design." *Byte* (April 1982): 108-132.

Smith, Robert Frederick. "A Funny Thing is Happening to the Library on the Way to the Future." *The Futurist* (April 1978): 85-91.

"Specifications for an Online Catalog." Chicago, IL: Consortium to Develop an Online Catalog (CONDOC), November 2, 1981.

Stevens, Norman D. "The Catalogs of the Future: A Speculative Essay." *Journal of Library Automation* 13 (2) (June 1980): 88-95.

Suprenant, Tom. "Future Libraries: The Electronic Environment." *Wilson Library Bulletin* (January 1982): 336-341.

Tenopir, Carol. "In-House Databases II: Evaluating and Choosing Software." *Library Journal* (May 1, 1983): 885-888.

Uluakar, Tamar; Pierce, Anton R. and Chacra, Vinod. "Design Principles for a Comprehensive Library System." *Library Automation* 14 (2) (June 1981): 80-89.

Van Pulis, Noelle. "User Education for an Online Catalog: A Workshop Approach." *Research Quarterly* (Fall 1981): 61-69.

White, Herb. "The Shock that Hurts." *American Libraries* (October 1980): 534-535.

Wright, William F. and Hawkins, Donald T. "Information Technology: A Bibliography." *Special Libraries* (April 1981): 163-71.

Zurkowski, Paul. "The Library Context and the Information Context: Bridging the Theoretical Gap." *Library Journal* (July 1981): 1381-1384.

Index

ABOUT THE AUTHOR

Emily Gallup Fayen is director of library automation at the Dartmouth College Baker Library, where she served as project leader and principal investigator for the Dartmouth On-Line Catalog Project and the Dartmouth On-Line Circulation Project. She was also coordinator for the Online Patron Access Project, sponsored by the Council on Library Resources. Previously, she was a programmer/analyst at the Norris Cotton Cancer Center at Dartmouth College. From 1972 to 1976 she was a consultant to the U.S. government on very large-scale online information storage and retrieval systems.

Ms. Fayen has been active as a consultant, speaker and writer of many articles and reports. She is coauthor of *Information Retrieval On-Line*, which won the Best Information Science Book Award of the American Society for Information Science, and *Four Approaches to the Man-Machine Interface*. A graduate of the University of Maryland, she holds an M.P.A. in information science from American University.